SUCCESS

IN THE NEW

RETIREMENT

SIX KEYS TO NAVIGATE THE NEW RETIREMENT

MATT DEATON

CONTRIBUTIONS BY DAMON ROBERTS

For Katie
My real compass.

*"An investment in knowledge
pays the best interest."*
— Benjamin Franklin

CONTENTS

Keys to Navigation

ACKNOWLEDGEMENTS

This book would not be in your hands without the help, expertise and kindness of so many. First, to all those who read drafts and made suggestions that improved and clarified the manuscript, especially Damon Roberts whose contributions have been indispensable, and April Price whose lack of financial knowledge was superseded by her ability to edit and untangle sentences.

A special thanks to Patrick Kelly, whose books and writing I have always admired, and who was gracious enough to read this book and offer his encouragement.

My dad wrote his first book when I was a boy and, as in all things, showed me the way to build a business and a career on my own terms. My parents have climbed mountain after mountain and I owe my ambition, initiative and confidence to them. The life I have created is a result of watching their steady footsteps.

And most especially, I want to recognize our clients who have trusted us with their most precious resources at the most critical time in their lives. Their stories and experiences have inspired and motivated me and I have learned invaluable lessons working with them. I count it as a great privilege to have the chance to navigate this journey together.

CHAPTER 1

NO ONE WILL CARE AS MUCH AS YOU WILL ABOUT YOUR MONEY

> *"It takes as much energy to wish as it does to plan."*
> — **Eleanor Roosevelt**

When I was a kid, I had a dream to one day play football for the Dallas Cowboys. I had big plans to be the next Danny White. So I got a book from the school library, *How to Play in the NFL*, and I read it over and over. It had lots of great tips on how to prepare for my future career in the NFL. And as I read and studied and memorized that book, I started setting goals and making changes in my life. I had a dream and I had a plan.

The hardest part was convincing my mom. If I was going to have any shot of making it to the NFL, we were going to have to make some serious changes around the house. One important tip in the book was that in addition to getting enough sleep and starting a rigorous exercise routine, I needed to make dietary changes, like eating lots of protein and drinking skim milk. My parents only drank whole milk. (This was the 80s after all.) I campaigned for weeks to get my mom to buy a different kind of milk and finally, harassed and worn down, she gave in. My career prospects were looking up! There were now two kinds of milk on our breakfast table: one for the future NFL quarterbacks and one for everyone else.

Now obviously, my dreams and plans changed over the years, but the point is that no one was going to care about my NFL hopes and dreams as much as me! No one was going to come by and hand me a football and a contract because they just really wanted me to have my dream career. My mom wasn't going to change the family's dairy habits without my constant begging and pestering. And Tom Landry wasn't going to call me up out of the blue and beg me to come to the Cowboys training camp because I was the missing link in their Super Bowl prospects. It was my dream, and if I wanted it, I would have to set the goals, drink the milk, put in the time, and make the sacrifices to get it.

The exact same principles apply to your retirement. Success in retirement depends on taking control of your finances, getting educated, and creating a plan. And no one is going to care about your plan, your money, and your retirement as much as you!

Instinctively, we all know this, of course. But on the long and winding path to retirement, we face obstacles and roadblocks and this can lead too many people to act like their retirement is something that will magically just happen. They forget that they are the one and only driving force that really cares about what happens to their money and can ensure a prosperous future.

The most common roadblock I see in my work every day is fear. Many people are overwhelmed and scared. They don't understand where to start or how to prepare and this leads to paralysis rather than action. They are uneducated about the varying investment vehicles and when to use them, mystified by the terms and the rules associated with these tools, and the tax consequences are like a foreign language. Above all, people are desperately worried about losing the money they have worked so hard to save.

Another common obstacle is that immediate needs frequently take precedence over future ones. This is just part of our DNA. Our caveman self sees no sense saving that meaty zebra bone for next week when we need the energy right now to run as fast as possible from the saber-tooth tiger. We address our current, pressing concerns at the expense of our future plans and this leads to missed opportunities, lost time to grow our money, and inadequate savings.

Creating a plan minimizes these hurdles and doubts, and this book was written to help you create that plan. Fear and paralysis can be addressed through education and action!

Understanding your options and the realities of retirement can help you take control of what happens to your money. The key is to get educated, set goals, and then follow through on your own personal plan for your own personal retirement.

I recently had some clients, a husband and wife, who came to see me. They had been married for ten years and this was a second marriage for both of them. They were both retired and the wife was ten years younger than her husband. The husband had retired a few years before they met, and because he was single at the time, he had claimed the single life pension from his company to maximize his income for as long as he lived. Unfortunately, this pension would stop when he passed away. The second marriage, as wonderful as it was, had changed the retirement plan.

His pension and Social Security benefits accounted for 70% of their retirement income, and with women statistically living longer than men, the odds of her outliving her husband and his income were very high. They weren't naive to their situation and, to their credit, they had been scrimping and saving everything they could, trying to build up some reserves to protect against the likely loss of income she would experience. They were putting off some of the "bucket list" items they had always wanted to do and the fear and pressure was starting to affect their marriage.

The good news is that they really had done a good job saving for retirement. Both had diligently funded their retirement accounts when they were working and had built an admirable nest egg. They had paid off their home and had no other debt.

They were better prepared than most and yet, when I met them, they were scared to death. They didn't know how they were going to replace his income and they were paralyzed with fear. The husband kept them on a very tight budget which didn't leave much room for the fun things that bring life meaning.

There was fear and worry because they didn't know what possible situations they would face in the future, nor have any kind of strategy for handling them. All of that changed when we sat down and made a plan.

Now, they could have just rolled the dice. They could have just hoped that he would somehow outlive his wife. Or they could have put their heads in the sand and pretended that she would somehow just figure it out when she got there, cross that proverbial bridge when she came to it. Maybe she'd find a new sweetheart that would take care of her or, as a last resort, move in with her kids. Hey, as long as we're dreaming, they could have hoped to just pass away peacefully in their sleep on the exact same day. Problem solved.

They could nervously hope, or they could make a plan.

Today many people have their retirement money socked away in 401(k)s and IRAs. Usually these funds are made up of a mix of mutual funds, stocks, and bonds, carefully chosen by estimating the average returns that we hope they will generate. We can hope that the market will be kind and remain stable so that we can access those funds at any time and generate whatever income we need. We can hope, crossing our fingers and toes, that we'll have enough money to last through retirement, but the reality is that we don't really know what the market is going to do and that uncertainty leads to fear and worry.

We can just hope for the best, or we can make a plan.

It's your retirement. No one will care about your money and how you spend your retirement years as much as you will. It's time to get educated, make a plan, and if necessary, change the milk you're drinking. This is your dream. And it's time to make it happen.

CHAPTER 2

THE CHANGING LANDSCAPE OF RETIREMENT

*"Change is the law of life.
And those who look only to
the past or present are certain
to miss the future."*
— **John F. Kennedy**

The old metaphor for retirement was the three-legged stool. For decades, the golden years of life for most Americans were supported and maintained by three equally dependable legs: Social Security, a pension, and savings. The stool was so sturdy, in fact, that many people lived comfortably on their pension and Social Security checks and used their savings for fun things like traveling and spoiling the grandchildren. I was one of those grandchildren…I'm telling you, those were great times!

When my grandfather retired in the 1980s, he retired early, received a healthy pension from the state and spent his days perfecting his golf game and traveling the United States with my grandmother in their comfortable motorhome. James and Shirley visited the Space Needle, Mount Rushmore, Independence Hall, and all the grandkids along the way, filling their tank without a care and enjoying their well-earned respite. When each grandchild turned twelve, we were invited to go on a trip with Grandma and Grandpa. I still remember my trip to Star Valley, Wyoming where my cousin and I spent a week exploring the river and mountains together and golfing everyday with Grandpa. It was the trip of a lifetime for a young boy.

Because of his healthy pension and Social Security benefits, my Grandpa began every month with Social Security and pension deposits in his checking account—his retirement protected and secure. Very little time was spent worrying about money which allowed him to spend his stress-free days doing what he loved with the people he loved.

Retirement is changing

Fast-forward twenty-five years, and my father's retirement is a completely different picture. As a member of the baby boomer generation, he (along with 80 million other Americans) is pioneering a new way to retire. Today, more and more baby boomers are retiring without a pension and most have concerns about the long-term strength of the Social Security program. As a result, for many retirees, two legs of that once sturdy stool are anything but "secure." For many, gone are the days of guaranteed retirement income streams.

To make matters worse, Americans are living longer. While this is obviously a good thing, baby boomers are trying to figure out how they are going to make their money last as long as they do. With a projected life span that is 14.5 years longer than their grandparents, this can be a daunting task. It's no wonder that survey after survey shows that the greatest fear of retirees today is outliving their money.

While things have changed, it's not necessarily bad news. Navigating a new way to retire has also produced more independence and choice. Both Social Security and pensions were designed with a specific retirement age in mind which limited when and how you could retire. Pensions generally had strict rules that required someone to work for a certain amount of years in order to receive the promised benefits. As a result, many remained in jobs they didn't enjoy, putting in their time to hit the "magic number" of years of service or meet age stipulations in order to receive their pension payout.

Social Security also has set payouts at defined ages. Follow the rules and everything was laid out for you. However, lose your job early, experience health problems, or make a job change, and it could result in lost benefits or reduced income streams.

Freedom and responsibility in today's retirement

Unlike those whose retirement date is determined by their employer, today most retirees have much more independence when it comes to retirement. Most retirement assets are now held in 401(k) or IRA accounts which gives each individual the power to elect how much to save, how to invest those assets, and when and how much to withdraw. Retirement is in your hands. You are in control.

But like most things, this increased freedom and flexibility comes at a price. The responsibility to create a successful retirement plan is now on you. It is up to you to determine what your retirement will look like and how prepared you will be. If a proper plan is not put in place, this new freedom can end up being a curse due to inadequate savings or poor investment decisions.

Never has there been a time where it is more vital to educate yourself and pay careful attention to what is happening to your money, your retirement, and your future.

Navigating the new retirement

As a teenager, my parents would always remind me that I could earn more freedom as I proved that I was responsible enough to handle it. (The time my friends and I decided it was a good idea to try parasailing behind my friend's family station wagon put a clamp on that extra freedom for a while, but that's a whole other story.) Whether or not we've earned it, retirement today is much the same.

The proverbial stool is now a world-class utility belt with a multitude of tools that can be used to customize a personal retirement, but it is up to you to learn how to use it and make it work for you. And while some would like to turn back the clock to "the good old days" when retirement was more assured and automatic, that longing won't actually get you any closer to your own carefree days on the golf course.

The key to a successful retirement is recognizing and accepting that the rules of the game have changed! As you will see in the next two chapters, major changes have impacted pensions and Social Security and more changes are on the way. Understanding the changing landscape of retirement is the first step to being prepared for what the future holds.

Retirement today is not hopeless or impossible. Different? Undoubtedly. But you can make the new landscape work for you. Recognize that things have changed and then get prepared. This will require becoming educated about new vehicles and strategies that can help you reach your retirement goals. Then, with the help of a trusted advisor, you can create a plan designed to help you get where you want to be when you punch that golden retirement ticket. With planning and knowledge, your retirement can be just as golden and carefree as my grandparents'.

CHAPTER 3

SOCIAL SECURITY SUSTAINABILITY

"We can never insure one hundred percent of the population against one hundred percent of the hazards and vicissitudes of life, but we have tried to frame a law which will give some measure of protection to the average citizen and to his family against the loss of a job and against poverty-ridden old age."

— Franklin Roosevelt's statement on signing the Social Security Act, 1935

When I was ten years old I worked two jobs before the school day even started. The first was a good, old-fashioned paper route. (I'm not even sure they have these anymore.)

My mom woke me and two of my brothers at 5am and drove us to the newspaper office where we would fold the papers, stuff our bags and then walk the dark streets of our little town delivering the newspaper. We delivered papers year-round—in the snow, in the rain, sick or tired, it didn't matter. Sundays were the hardest, as our bags weighed twice as much and could only hold half the papers. My mom would drop another bag filled with the rest of the Sunday papers at a strategic location along the route because we couldn't carry them all.

On weekdays, after we finished the paper route, we'd head to my dad's dental office where we were paid to clean it every morning—empty the garbage, vacuum the floors, clean the bathrooms, and disinfect all the sinks and counters in the office. On the weekends my brothers and I would do the landscaping for the medical complex where my dad's office was located.

I learned early that if I wanted to have money, I had to get up and work for it.

Which is all well and good when you're a young, healthy, ten-year-old with strength and stamina and energy to burn. But, you can't deliver papers and mow lawns until the day you die. There is a point at which labor for your daily bread is no longer feasible or even possible.

The New Deal

When Social Security was first created the nation was at a crossroads. In the years leading up to its enactment, the country had transitioned from an agrarian society to an industrial nation. Families were no longer supporting each other on family farms from cradle to grave. The US was in the midst of the Great Depression and poverty was rampant, particularly among the elderly population. The Roosevelt administration was inundated with letters of suffering and requests for help.

Interesting Facts

- The first Social Security number was issued in November of 1936. Since then, 453.7 million numbers have been issued.
- Ida May Fuller was the first person to receive monthly payments of $22.53 from Social Security.

In response, the Social Security Act was created by President Franklin D. Roosevelt in 1935 and was designed to be self-sustaining. It was devised as a social insurance plan rather than a welfare program. Taxpayers would pay into the system through the payroll tax and be able to collect monthly benefit payments at retirement age. In many ways it is similar to buying a government bond; you give the government your money to hold for a while, and you receive it back at a low rate of return when you retire. The money is kept safe by the full faith and credit of the United States government.

The money you have paid into Social Security has accumulated through a payroll tax of 12.4%, 6.2% being paid by you, and 6.2% being paid by your employer. (Of course, if you are self-employed, you get the distinct pleasure of paying all of it yourself.) Since the first payments were made over 70 years ago, over $14 trillion in income has been collected by the SSA and almost $12 trillion has been paid out to recipients. Today, the average monthly benefit for an individual is $1,406 and the average couple receives $2,260 per month. The maximum monthly Social Security benefit payment for a person retiring in 2017 at full retirement age is $2,687, provided the person earned the maximum taxable earnings ($127,200 in 2017) for at least 35 working years. The benefit is intended to replace about 40-60% of an individual's income when they retire.

Is it going to disappear?

At the inception of the program, there were few beneficiaries in comparison with the number of workers contributing to the fund. In the early 50s, there were nearly 16 workers per retiree. But as birth rates decline and baby boomers retire, the worker-to-beneficiary ratio is decreasing, estimated at only 3.0 in 2015 and continuing to drop. With more than

59 million Americans receiving Social Security benefits, Social Security's expenses currently exceed the income it generates from payroll taxes. Over the next fifteen years, as the baby boomers retire en masse, the amount of Social Security recipients is expected to exceed 85 million. From now until 2030, it is projected that the number of people eligible for Social Security benefits will increase by 65%, while the number of people paying Social Security taxes will only grow by 15%.

THE POPULATION IS AGING

| 1950 (16:1) | 1960 (5:1) | 2015 (3:1) | 2035 (2:1) |

>>THE NUMBER OF WORKERS PER SOCIAL SECURITY RETIREE IS FALLING

Source: 2016 Social Security Trustees Report

This increase in the number of individuals receiving Social Security benefits compared to those that are contributing into the fund puts strain on the financial stability of the program. It is expected that over the next 15 years the excess money in the Social Security Trust Fund will be reduced gradually until it runs out by the end of the year 2032.

If changes are not made, the program will not remain solvent, and significant reductions in Social Security payments or other drastic measures will have to be taken.

Lessons from 1983

Keeping Social Security afloat is not a new problem. In 1983, the Reagan administration made changes to the program to ensure that benefits would continue for retirees and restore Social Security's solvency.

- Payroll taxes gradually increased from 8.05% to 12.4%.
- The retirement age was also gradually increased, from age 65 to age 67. An individual could still claim early retirement benefits at age 62 but the benefits were reduced by a greater amount.
- The delayed retirement credit was increased in gradual steps from 3% up to as high as 8%.
- Beginning in 1984 and depending on income, Social Security benefits were now taxable. (This one provision alone was estimated to cover 30% of the future shortfall in funding.)

While the amendments of 1983 did much to keep Social Security out of the red and viable for many years, it is clear that the program is vulnerable once again and more changes are on the horizon.

The changes have already begun

In December of 2015, Congress passed a budget agreement that included language that ended the ability of most individuals to employ certain Social Security spousal-claiming strategies. The bill eliminated or modified the popular "File and Suspend" and "Restricted Spousal" strategies which were available for those individuals who delayed claiming Social Security until they reached full retirement age. While these changes will save the program some money, the question remains as to what other changes are necessary to ensure the financial future of Social Security.

More changes are needed

The 2016 Social Security Trustee Report contains a statement that makes it very clear that additional changes are necessary if Social Security is going to remain viable:

> "If substantial actions are deferred for several years, the changes necessary to maintain Social Security solvency would be concentrated on fewer years and fewer generations... The Trustees recommend that lawmakers address the projected trust fund shortfalls in a timely way in order to phase in necessary changes gradually and give workers and beneficiaries time to adjust to them.

19

Implementing changes sooner rather than later would allow more generations to share in the needed revenue increases or reductions in scheduled benefits and could preserve more trust fund reserves to help finance future benefits."

None of the necessary changes are going to be popular but delaying the inevitable is only going to make the cuts deeper and more painful. Sometimes it's just better to rip the bandage off.

So, what are our options?

While we can't predict the exact changes coming to Social Security, looking at current proposals can help us anticipate the impact these changes may have on our own retirement plans. Similar to the changes in 1983, the best options for keeping Social Security solvent include raising payroll taxes, increasing retirement ages, and modifying how cost-of-living adjustments are determined.

Increase the Payroll Tax

Currently, the payroll tax is 12.4% (6.2% contributed by both you and your employer) and has been the same since 1990, except for a temporary "payroll tax holiday" in 2010 and 2011 when the payroll tax was reduced by 2%. One proposal recommends increasing the payroll tax gradually, by 0.1% per year for 20 years until it reaches 14.4%, eliminating 49% of the shortfall.

Raise the Retirement Age

In January of 2012, the Congressional Budget Office issued a report that stated raising the full retirement age to age 70 by two months per year for anyone born after 1960 would cover nearly half of the expected shortfall. With life expectancy increasing and more people working longer, this may be a viable solution to extend the program. Even less aggressive increases in retirement age could make big impacts on the solvency of the program.

Reduce Cost-Of-Living Allowances (COLAs)

When Social Security was first created, there was not an automatic system in place to increase benefits paid due to inflation, otherwise known as cost-of-living adjustments (COLAs). When Ida May Fuller received her first monthly payment of $22.54 in 1940, it remained the same for the next 10 years. In 1950, the first increase to existing benefits occurred. This increase and all future increases were approved only through special acts of Congress which were very inconsistent and difficult to plan around. In 1972, the law was amended to provide for automatic COLAs based on the consumer price index. A proposal has been put forth that would tie COLAs to a new inflation index called the chained CPI. This index assumes that consumers change their purchasing habits when prices increase. This change would decrease future COLAs and result in potential savings of as much as 6%.

The long and short of it

This much we know: changes to Social Security are coming. Without some adjustments the program is not sustainable. The challenge is predicting what changes will actually be made. While the actual revisions Congress may make remain a bit cloudy and unpredictable, it is safe to assume that the likely amendments will include some form of or combination of these current proposals. Understanding and anticipating these changes and then adjusting your financial plan to maximize the benefits you can receive will be a critical step in developing a comprehensive financial plan.

Maximizing your benefits

While it may feel like what happens to Social Security is largely out of your control, one area you can manage and use to your advantage is deciding how and when you claim your benefits. Keep in mind that taking benefits before your full retirement age will reduce your benefits by as much as 30%. On the other hand, if you can delay taking your benefits until after your full retirement age you can increase your benefit by 8% per year. Depending on life expectancy, your personal health and situation, how you claim Social Security benefits can result in a difference of tens of thousands of dollars over your lifetime or the life of your spouse.

Everyone's situation is different. There are different claiming strategies for married, unmarried, divorced, or widowed individuals. There are also strategies for starting and stopping a benefit in the case of temporary unemployment. Make sure that you understand all the benefits and options that are available to you and then make informed, calculated decisions in the context of your overall retirement plan.

I have a client that had a plan to continue working and wait as long as possible to claim her Social Security benefits. Then she lost her job. Rather than panic and start her Social Security benefit, we looked at the whole situation. She was old enough to claim the restricted spousal benefit through her ex-husband (this is no longer an option for those who are not already 62) and she acquired a part-time job. This gave her enough income to be able wait to claim her full retirement benefit, which will produce thousands of extra dollars in income over her lifetime.

While there have been changes to the Social Security program over the years and undoubtedly there will be more in the future, taking steps to maximize your benefits will only help you to be better positioned for a successful retirement. Regardless of future changes, Social Security will remain a critical part of your retirement strategy and it is vital that you take steps to make the most of the money you have contributed over your working career from your first job to your last.

CHAPTER 4

THE DISAPPEARING PENSION

*"In a world where people are living
longer and inflation is certain,
those [pension] promises will be
anything but easy to keep."*
— **Warren Buffett**

When I was a kid my dad introduced us to one of his all-time favorite movies, *It's a Mad, Mad, Mad, Mad World*. I remember him watching that movie, laughing so hard that tears streamed down his cheeks. At the heart of the movie, was Spencer Tracy, who played an old detective, Captain Culpepper. It was Culpepper's last day on the job and he was chasing a group of people who were racing to find some buried money from a crime committed early in

Culpepper's career. He had worked long and hard for the Santa Rosita Police Department, and in the middle of the movie, on his last day of work before retirement, he finds out his pension is gone. He is so devastated by this news, he walks out of the police department and joins this crazy mob of criminals in the final dash for the missing money.

As a kid, I didn't really get it. I didn't understand what Culpepper was so upset about, what a discovery like that would do to you on the doorstep of retirement. Now I appreciate the gravity and desperation of the situation. As funny as the film was, a disappearing pension is no laughing matter. And too many people find themselves in that very situation today.

After years of counting on their pensions to provide income for the rest of their lives, many are discovering that the assumptions that were made are failing, mismanagement is being revealed, and the chickens are coming home to roost. Unfortunately, retirees are the ones paying the price. A new reality has started to set in. Pensions aren't as secure as promised. Some may fail, while others may require drastic cuts or restructuring. The disappearing pension is a major factor in the changing retirement landscape.

A bit of a history lesson

Back in the "good old days" landing a job with a pension was considered the golden ticket to retirement. The promised pension would provide a guaranteed stream of income throughout retirement for the employee and in return the employer was able to use the "golden handcuffs" to keep employees longer and reduce turnover. For decades, this system provided tangible benefits for both the employer and employee, and along with Social Security benefits, shaped the way Americans retired. In 1980, almost 100% of public employees and over 80% of private employees were covered by a *defined benefit* pension plan. Life was good.

Around this same time a major shift in the way Americans would retire began when the first 401(k), a *defined contribution* plan, was put in place in 1981. Instead of the company funding a "defined benefit" that would provide a specified amount of retirement income to the employee, the employee would now be able to "contribute" into a tax-deferred account and the employer could match or supplement those contributions. As we talked about in Chapter 2, this shift has brought more independence and flexibility when it comes to retirement but also more individual responsibility.

Percentage of employees participating in defined benefit pension plans, private industry, for selected years during 1981–2011

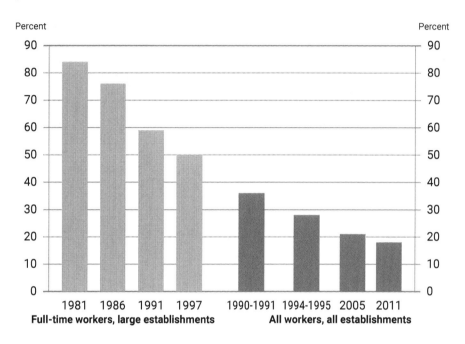

NOTE: Information shown for 1990–1991 and 1994–1995 uses combined data from separate surveys of small and large private establishments

SOURCE: U.S. Bureau of Labor Statistics

Assumptions failed

When a company or public entity sets up a pension plan, the employer guarantees a defined or specified amount of benefit during retirement. This specified amount is usually determined using a formula that factors in years of employment and the employee's earnings. Behind the scenes, the company must make some key assumptions that will be used to determine how much money needs to be set aside to fulfill these obligations, including an estimated rate of return on the pension assets, estimated retirement ages, and life expectancy. Make the correct assumptions and the promised benefits will be paid out over the life of the employee. Make the wrong assumptions and the funds needed to meet the promised obligations just won't be there.

Rate of Return

Rate of return is one of the most critical assumptions made in a pension plan because it has such a dramatic impact on the assets available to meet the promised benefits. The big problem with this is that most pension funds were set up during times when interest rates and market returns were much higher. When interest rates were higher, pension funds were able to achieve a more consistent rate of return because they could allocate funds to more conservative, predictable investments. As interest rates have declined, pension funds have been forced to take additional risks in an effort to achieve the necessary returns. The added risk has increased the volatility of fund performance, often resulting in poor returns.

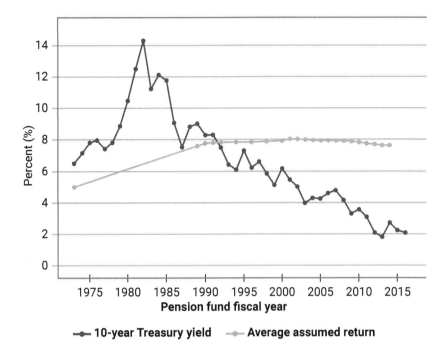

Source: The Rockefeller Institute of Government[1]

According to the National Association of State Retirement Administrators, US pension plans are estimating an average return of 7.6% even though interest rates remain at historical lows. This aggressive assumption has proven to be impossible to achieve. For example, in 2016, CalPERS, the California public pension fund, announced that over the previous year they only achieved a return of .61% which fell well short of their projected rate of return of 7.5%.[2]

In addition to weak returns, pensions are susceptible to mismanagement. The Dallas Police and Fire Pension, which covers nearly 10,000 first responders, is on the verge of collapse because of sketchy fund management.

Starting in 2005, the fund's investment manager moved over 50% of the fund's assets out of the stock market and into real estate and other "hard assets." By the time this "diversification" was complete, investments included luxury apartment buildings, Hawaiian homes, a tract of undeveloped land in the Arizona desert, and Uruguayan timber. The problem was that the fund manager had complete discretion over how these "illiquid" investments were valued on the books. When the financial assets were examined by new fund managers in 2015, they were uncomfortable with the overvaluations and DPFP was forced to mark down its entire real estate book by 32%, putting the entire fund at risk of insolvency.

Even though interest rates have declined dramatically, assumed investment returns have increased or remained level. This means pension funds must allocate more funds to investments with risk in order to achieve the assumed rate of return.

Estimated Retirement Age

Estimating when an employee will begin to take benefits is another key assumption of a successful pension plan. Estimated retirement age along with life expectancy estimates allow a fund to accurately estimate how much will be paid out to each employee and how much must be set aside. Pension laws are fairly lax on how these assumptions are determined stating only that assumptions "must be reasonable."

To help control this variable, most plans put rules in place that required a minimum age or years of service before becoming eligible. Unfortunately, these rules were not always effective. There are multiple examples of failed pension plans where companies made incorrect assumptions on how these rules would be applied.

Planes, trains, and automobiles

For example, US Airways decided it was "reasonable" to assume their pilots would retire at age 60, the same age the FAA grounds commercial pilots. Their spokesman said, "Pilots enjoy flying...A lot of pilots would even work past 60 if they could." When the US Airways pilot pension plan failed in 2003, it was discovered that more than half of their pilots were retiring well before age 60. I guess it wasn't as fun to fly planes as the company thought.

The US Airways case shows how dramatically a pension plan can be affected by assumptions that look only "slightly off the mark." By assuming the pilots would retire four years later than they actually did, US Airways had a shortfall of $385 million which resulted in the pension's collapse.

Incorrect assumptions about retirement age were also the determining factors in the collapse of the Bethlehem Steel and CNF Trucking pensions, where employees could retire with full pension benefits after hitting 30 years of service, regardless of age. These plans made the faulty assumption that younger employees would continue to work even after they were eligible to retire. It's hard to believe these companies assumed people just loved their jobs so much they would want to work longer than they had to. You'd think a basic understanding of human nature would help them figure out this theory was faulty.

Life Expectancy

Because pensions pay employees "income for life," how long those employees are expected to live is a critical factor in pension fund managment. Obviously, the longer a person lives the more money they will need from the pension fund. As a result, the life expectancy number a plan uses will directly affect the estimated pension liabilities, which in turn will determine the needed contribution amounts.

Over the past 50 years, life expectancy has increased dramatically and is expected to continue to increase. I'm happy to report that my grandpa has lived well past the life expectancy assumptions of his state pension plan. At 92 and kicking, James continues to collect a pension check from the state and, thankfully, shows no signs of giving up his benefit anytime soon. While some funds have adjusted their estimates to prepare for employees living longer, many have been slow to respond.

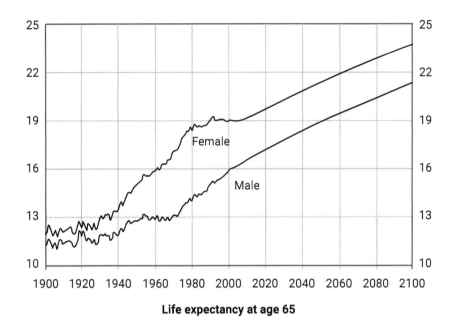

Life expectancy at age 65

Source: Social Security Administration[3]

It is estimated that for each year of life expectancy the estimated pension liability increases by around 4-5%.[4] To put it differently, the most stable pension funds use higher or more conservative life expectancy assumptions. The pension funds that chose to use lower life expectancy estimates are dealing with significant funding shortfalls.

Illinois, New York, and GM, for starters

Illinois now has the worst-funded pensions of any state, with the accounts holding about 42% of what's needed to fulfill pension obligations. The combination of early retirement and longer life expectancy have resulted in the average state pensioner spending 24 years working for the state and then drawing pension benefits for an estimated 26 years. The assumptions were so far off, one out of every five Illinois state pensioners will receive over $2 million in lifetime pension benefits, and over half of pensioners will receive $1 million or more—amounts far larger than what the average private-sector employee can ever hope to receive from Social Security.

There is a similar problem in New York City, where police and firefighters can retire after 20 years of service, but are estimated to live into their 80s on average. This means that pension checks might be collected for 40 years, resulting in benefits of over $2 million per person. With over 10,000 cops in their 40s currently collecting pension benefits, as Buffett said, that's a promise that's going to be hard to keep.

Longer lifespans have not only impacted public pensions, things are no easier in corporate America. The Society of Actuaries released new mortality tables in October of 2014 increasing lifespans by 2 years since the last update in 2000, and just a few months later, that impact was felt in fourth-quarter earnings statements across Wall Street. General Motors, for example, reported that the new mortality data added $2.2 billion to its already underfunded pension liabilities.

The aftermath of failed assumptions

As a result of these failed assumptions, many pensions are underfunded. The Hoover Insitution estimates that even using the unrealistic rate of return of 7.6% for future returns, public pensions are still $1.2 trillion underfunded. Private pensions are in the same leaky boat, with estimates putting their deficit at $343 billion in unfunded liabilties.[5]

The result of these deficits on public pensions will likely be cuts, limits on cost-of-living adjustments (COLAs) and increased taxes. For example, Chicago recently approved a new tax on water usage, the biggest tax increase in recent memory, to make up their current pension shortfall which is currently only 32% funded.

Private companies, on the other hand, are getting rid of pensions. Because of the large burden on company finances and shareholders, many pensions have been eliminated or grandfathered out and replaced by defined contribution plans. Other solutions include offering employees a lump sum payout or an annuity in place of the pension.

What about my guarantees?

Private pensions are insured and protected by the federal Pension Benefit Guaranty Corporation (PBGC). This independent agency of the US government insures pension benefits are paid even if the employer fails to pay the required premiums. If a pension plan ends without sufficient funds to pay all the benefits promised, PBGC will pay the promised benefit provided by the pension plan, "up to the limits set by law."[6] In 2015, those limits were set at $60,136 for 65-year-old retirees on a single-employer plan and $12,870 for those on a multiemployer plan.

Corporations pay a premium every year to the PBCG in order to insure their pension plans. But the increasing pressures on the PBCG to cover failing pension plans has put the agency in the red. Premium costs are expected to rise 25% over the next four years to try and address the shortfall, which is currently underfunded by $76 billion and has more than doubled since 2013. This is clearly a troubling trend.

PBGC's Net Financial Position of the Single-Employer and Multiemployer Programs Combined[7]

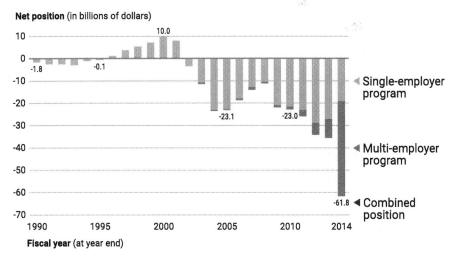

Source: Pension Benefit Guaranty Corporation (PBGC) | GAO-15-290

37

Life imitates art

It turns out that Captain Culpepper's calamity was not so far-fetched. If you currently have a pension, this should be a wakeup call that at some point you may find yourself relying on your 401(k), IRA, or other investment savings to fund your income in retirement. If you don't have a pension, while funding your retirement is entirely your responsibility, you should also recognize that you have complete control over your nest egg and you can avoid those unpleasant "surprises" that are likely in many pensioners' futures. Either way, your retirement accounts and savings are essential to your retirement and it is critically important to make the best decisions to grow and protect them. It's either that or go look for buried treasure. I hear there's some under "a big W." (And if you haven't seen *It's a Mad, Mad, Mad, Mad World*, you really need to take some time this weekend to watch it. You'll thank me.)

CHAPTER 5

THE GROUND RULES OF INVESTING

"There's no crying in baseball or investing."
— **Jill Schlesinger**

have five brothers and we grew up playing baseball together. There was always enough of us to put together some sort of game, with the game of choice being "Over-the-Line." We spent all of our free time on the makeshift diamonds of our backyard and the empty greenspace across the street. No matter how hot the Arizona summer got, we were out there.

Over-the-line is normally played on a beach and has its own set of rules, so because we were playing it in our yard, we modified the rules quite a bit. Like baseball, the goal was to score as many runs as possible. The tricky part was that to get a hit you had to hit the ball "over the line," an imaginary line where the outfield started. If the ball landed over the line, the batter could continue to run, but had to be standing on a base by the time the other team got the ball back across the line. Even if you had a good hit, if you tried to stretch it into a double or triple and the other team got the ball back over the line before you reached the base, you were out. It was our park, our rules. And we all knew them.

Occasionally, though, we'd talk one of our friends or neighbors into joining the game. There was always a bit of a learning curve with our ground rules and I'm pretty sure we never really explained them all. It didn't take long for the new kid to get called out because he wasn't standing on a base when the ball crossed back over the line.

There are also a few ground rules to investing—a few things you should know and be aware of before you get called out on your way around the bases or struck out before you even start.

The third leg

After reading the chapters on Social Security and pensions, it should be pretty clear that there's a lot riding on the third leg of that proverbial stool. If you are like most retirees you will rely heavily on your retirement savings to close the gap between what guaranteed income streams cover and the rest of the income you will need during retirement. Therefore, protecting and growing that nest egg is critically important.

Because succeeding is so important in retirement and the potential missteps are so plentiful, investing your life savings can be a very intimidating undertaking for anyone. Whether it's at the office, in the school parking lot, or on the sidelines at my son's little league game, when people find out what I do, they immediately ask the question, "What should I be doing with my money?" There's a pretty common feeling out there that nobody really knows how or where they should be investing, and they're pretty sure that wherever they're invested, it's probably the wrong place. They're also pretty sure they could be doing better somewhere else, if only they had the inside scoop.

There is no one-size-fits-all answer. It's not something you can answer with a glib response between plays at a Pop Warner game. "Oh, what you want is the Magic Wonder Fund...you haven't heard of that? Amazing returns, no risk. Put it there and you'll be fine...never have to think about it again." If only it were that easy.

The inherent problem with investing

If you could always pick the next Google or Amazon your investments would provide significant returns with very few losses. But picking the stocks that are going to be winners is a proposition that sometimes involves as much chance as a weekend in Vegas. In the same summer that "bookseller" Amazon went public, another online retailer, OnSale—which sold everything from computer supplies to Omaha steaks—also went public. They were only separated by $2 at their initial public offering and OnSale generated a lot more excitement and press as an online bidding site than the tame, online bookseller did. Yet, today Amazon's stock has split three times and made its original investors very wealthy, while OnSale is no longer in existence, and chances are that you've probably never even heard of it. But in the summer of 1997 there was no way to predict which one would be which.

Bruce Arians, the head coach for the Arizona Cardinals, uses the phrase "No risk it, no biscuit" to describe his offensive approach to football. However, this may not be the best approach to investing when you are talking about your hard-earned money and your retirement nest egg. For Arians, there is always next week's game or next year's season to get another chance for a win. When it comes to our retirement money, we often don't get many second chances and the money lost on one bad investment can be very difficult to recover from.

The inherent problem of investing is that you have so little control over the outcomes that it sometimes bears more resemblance to "speculating" than "investing." Of course this is all considered just "part of the game" in the investment world. Managers just shrug their shoulders, "We're not going to get it right all the time. You win some, you lose some." In the dismal last days of 2008, one hedge fund, Greenlight Capital, sent a letter to its shareholders trying to explain the poor performance of the third quarter. They signed off the letter with the dismissive quote: "There's no crying in baseball." To be so nonchalant after dramatically shrinking their investors' savings was appallingly insulting, but, unfortunately, not extraordinary.

No one's going to care more about your money than you are. And that is never more true than when we are talking about investing.

The value proposition

At the end of the day, investing should be evaluated based on a value proposition, with the four key components being rate of return, how much risk is taken, the fees associated with the investment, and the amount you keep after taxes—How much risk am I taking? What returns did I receive by taking that risk? How much did it cost me? How much did I actually get to keep?

Unfortunately, too many investors only look at the returns they get and ignore the amount of risk it took to generate that return.

For example, if you have two portfolios that both generate an 8% return but one does it with half the risk, which one would you choose? Obviously we would all choose the one with the same return but lower risk. But what would you do if you have two portfolios where one generates a 7% return and one generates an 8% return but the one that generated the 7% return took half the risk of the other. Now the decision becomes a little more complicated.

Depending on your risk tolerance and investment goals, you may choose the portfolio with the lower rate of return because the reduced risk adds "value" to your investment objectives. At the end of the day, you may have received a slightly lower monetary return but the reduced volatility allowed you to sleep at night.

The other component of the value proposition that many people ignore is the amount of fees they are paying. Too often returns are dramatically reduced over the life of the investment due to the constant drag of fees on the portfolio. (See Chapter 11 for a complete discussion on fees.) You must constantly ask the questions, "Am I getting my money's worth? Am I getting value?"

For example, let's take two portfolios. The first investment produces returns similar to the benchmark and the fee is .5% each year. The second portfolio has a fee of 2% but has consistently produced a return of 3% above the benchmark after fees. Which one would you choose?

Now before you answer don't forget to ask about the risk of the investment. (See, I almost got you there.) In this example, even though you would pay more in fees, the returns of the second portfolio are still better after the fees are subtracted. If the risk to each portfolio is the same, you could make the determination that the strategy of the second portfolio resulted in a better "value" even though it actually cost more.

At the end of the day, we should all be seeking a portfolio that produces the best return, with the lowest amount of risk, at the lowest cost possible. Finding the most efficient balance of these components is the key to a successful investment strategy.

Finally, all investment returns should be evaluated for their tax implications. If you get great returns for little risk at a low fee, but end up giving a chunk of it to Uncle Sam because it was not done tax efficiently, it may not meet your value proposition criteria. Anything that cuts into your returns—whether it's in fees or in taxes—must be carefully weighed to ensure that you are maximizing the value you received compared to the risk you took. We will talk more about tax implications in Chapter 12, but as we lay out the various investment options you can choose from to grow your nest egg, keep this value proposition in mind.

Emotional costs

The other day a retired gentleman came up to me in the hallway at church and said, "I've got a little bit of money, not much, but a little, and I'm not sure what to invest it in. Let me ask you this, how much of your money do you have in CDs?" He was so paralyzed by fear of losing his nest egg that he was unable to imagine putting it anywhere riskier than a CD, despite the abominable, nearly-negative returns on CDs. His emotions were running his investment show.

At the same time I meet with people every day that seem to have forgotten how they felt in 2008 when the markets were falling. The other day I was making this point with a client. I pulled up the performance of the S&P 500 over a ten year period beginning in 2006. Over that period of time, the S&P 500 produced a 5.26% return without dividends and 7.47% with dividends included. I asked the client if he would have been satisfied with the return over that 10-year period. Predictably, he said, "I wouldn't complain if it was more, but, yes, I would be happy with that." I then asked how he would feel if at one point during this ten-year period, his portfolio was down over 50%! He sort of shrugged his shoulders implying that he was fine with that big of a drop as long as he achieved those average returns in the end.

The problem is that it is human nature to "forget" about the pain or emotion we experience while going through a difficult experience. Have you ever heard a mother talk about her pregnancy? I heard my wife say "I am never doing this again" several times during each of her pregnancies with our three children. And who could blame her? I would have been in the fetal position for nine straight months. Immediately after giving birth the thought of having another child was just about the furthest thing from her mind. But as the months and years passed, the pain and discomfort of the pregnancy were now in the rear-view mirror and the joy and happiness of having a sweet, little baby was causing her to think, "It really wasn't that bad. We should do that again. It was totally worth it."

We do the same "emotional smoothing" when it comes to our investments. Because we can look back in hindsight and see that our accounts generated a healthy return we forget about the gut-wrenching, cold sweat, ulcer-inducing times that left us weak and panicky as our money rode the hideous ups and downs of the market. In hindsight, we look at those previous losses with the knowledge that our account recovered, and we say to ourselves, "See? It was worth taking those risks because look at my account balance today!"

However, in the midst of real-time, actual market downturns, we don't know if the drop is only temporary. We don't have the comfort of looking back on a nice, clean average rate of return when we are seeing our accounts drop by thousands of dollars on a daily basis.

We must recognize that we are emotional creatures and often those emotions can creep into our investment strategies. How our accounts are performing determines where we are in the "emotional cycle." Then, because our emotions have muddied the water, we don't always make the best decisions. Investment decisions should be made independently of emotion and should be based on reason. They should always be made with a plan in mind.

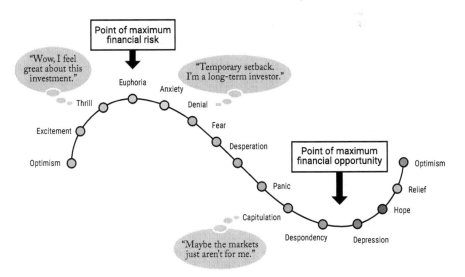

That said, one of the most underrated aspects of a properly designed portfolio is the effect that reduced volatility has on your ability to remain committed to an investment strategy. While meeting with clients, I will often ask them to draw a line showing me how they want their account to perform. In almost every case the client will draw a straight line trending upwards. In other words, they are looking for consistent growth on their account without a lot of ups and downs. As their advisor, the closer I can have their portfolio perform according to this expectation, the happier my clients will be and the more likely they will be to stay committed to the recommended investment strategy.

To achieve a more consistent rate of return means that not everything in your portfolio should be invested the same or with the same risk. As you will see in subsequent chapters, by understanding all your options and their accompanying risks, and then making decisions based on your own value proposition, you can develop a properly allocated portfolio you can live with.

CHAPTER 6

SECURITIES

Successful investing is about managing risk, not avoiding it.
— Benjamin Graham

Did you hear about the New York high school student who made $72 million by trading stocks on his lunch hour? It's a good story. A rags-to-riches, if-at-first-you-don't-succeed, anybody-can-do-it-with-the-right-amount-of-guts-brains-and-luck story. The story goes that the 17-year-old first invested his tutoring money in penny stocks when he was 9. Things did not go well and he lost a huge chunk of his money. Devastated by his loss, he thought he was done investing. But then, he started studying the titans of modern finance and found inspiration to try again and not be paralyzed by his loss. After all, as the experts say, "You learn more from your losses than from your gains."

That was the turning point. After that, he pulled himself up by his bootstraps and made $72 million. While many were floundering through the crash and recovery of the market over the last ten years, this kid was making a killing. The story appeared in both New York Magazine and the New York Post. Trouble was, none of it was true. Well, except for the losses in the penny market at age 9. That part you can believe.

How do these stories get published? Aren't there some glaring credibility gaps prompting writers and publishers to say, "Wait, a minute..."? The trouble is that when it comes to the stock market, there is a healthy myth out there that anyone (and everyone) can make it rich if they only had the right amount of knowledge and luck. We are all just one right pick away from making it big. And that myth just keeps getting bigger and bigger: It's easy. So easy, a high-schooler can do it. Stop being paralyzed by fear and just allow yourself to earn $72 million on your lunch break, geez.

The truth is that investing in securities is not easy. And as you approach retirement, there's a lot more at risk than your tutoring money. Understanding more about the vehicles and investment strategies that are available will help you make better decisions, manage your expectations, and reduce downside risk. Hopefully, armed with a little more knowledge, you will need a little less luck, because I can't help you there.

The investment backdrop

In the early days of the stock market, back when Wall Street was young, investment options were fairly simple and limited mostly to individual stocks and bonds. The market moved slowly because it was restricted by technology and the speed of information. You needed a lot of capital to be able to buy into the market. For example, when General Motors went public in 1910, it cost $33 per share, which translates into $800 per share in today's dollars.

Investing was also riskier because diversification was difficult due to the small number of publicly traded companies, lack of access to foreign markets, and the amount of money it took to invest in individual stocks. In 1920 it would have taken nearly $1700 in today's dollars to buy one share of General Motors and one share of Coca Cola. Trading your holdings was also more difficult and expensive because it was done in person on the floor of the stock exchange with physical stock certificates. As a result, when people bought stocks and bonds, they would generally buy and hold their investments for a long time.

Mutual funds: A solution with limitations

Over time, and in an effort to provide more diversification and make trading easier and cheaper, the mutual fund* was created. The first one, The Massachusetts Investors' Trust, went public in 1928. Rather than being limited to individual stocks or bonds, investors could now choose from professionally managed funds that were essentially a collection of various stocks or bonds. Mutual funds allowed people to invest with less capital and get more diversification while reducing trading costs due to economies of scale. Today there are over 14,000 mutual funds available.

While mutual funds have made the stock market more accessible to the average investor, they also have limitations that make them less nimble than other investment vehicles. First, when a mutual fund is created, paperwork must be filed with the SEC stating what types of investments that fund will invest in. The SEC also requires the name of the fund to describe the investment holding. For example, if you

---

* Mutual funds and Exchange Traded Funds (ETF's) are sold by prospectus. Please consider the investment objectives, risks, charges, and expenses carefully before investing. The prospectus, which contains this and other information about the investment company, can be obtained from the Fund Company or your financial professional. Be sure to read the prospectus carefully before deciding whether to invest.

have ever looked through the investment options offered in your 401(k) plan, you likely saw fund names with key words like "growth," "value," "blended." A fund that has the description of being a "growth stock fund" must hold at least 80% in growth stocks. This means that even though the fund is actively managed, the fund manager is limited by this label as to how the funds can be invested.

This limitation is critical to understand because it can have a great impact on your investment returns. For example, let's take the Fidelity Growth Company Fund. Let's say the team that manages that fund has been doing their job— analyzing their holdings, performing technical analysis, and monitoring market indicators. I mean you are paying fees for their services, so they better pick the very best investments, right?

If, after all of this effort, the data tells them that growth stocks are overvalued and a correction is likely, they would be limited on how much they could adjust the portfolio to protect your investment. Because they are required to keep 80% invested in growth assets, even though the data is screaming "sell," the fund managers' hands are tied. They can only do so much.

Another limitation of a mutual fund is that the value of a mutual fund (Net Asset Value or NAV) is calculated at the end of the trading day. For example, let's say you decide to sell your holding in a mutual fund at 11:00am when the fund is valued at $100 per share. Your sell order doesn't actually occur until the end of the day, at the value that is calculated after the close of market. This means that by the time the sell price is calculated it could be far lower than when you put in your sell request. During a volatile market, this disparity can be dramatic and can result in additional losses.

When mutual funds were originally created, they were actually considered a lower cost trading option but as technology has improved and information has become easier to obtain, mutual funds have started to lose their low-cost advantages. In fact, in many cases, mutual funds have some of the highest fees, which have impacted their ability to beat benchmark returns.

Rise of the ETF

A little more than twenty years ago, the limitations of mutual funds led to the rise of another investment vehicle: the ETF.* ETFs, or exchange-traded funds, are a basket

---

* Mutual funds and Exchange Traded Funds (ETF's) are sold by prospectus. Please consider the investment objectives, risks, charges, and expenses carefully before investing. The prospectus, which contains this and other information about the investment company, can be obtained from the Fund Company or your financial professional. Be sure to read the prospectus carefully before deciding whether to invest.

of diversified funds—a fund full of holdings. When most ETFs are created, a basket of holdings is picked and then zero or very few changes are ever made to those holdings, which makes them perform like an index. They give an investor the advantage of being liquid because they can be traded throughout the day and the price changes as they are bought and sold. Unlike mutual funds, ETFs are directly bought and sold on the secondary market (stock exchange), much like any other stock.

ETFs have very low fees because of the limited transactions. They are available in almost every asset class—stocks, bonds, real estate, commodities, currencies, etc.—and hold significantly more funds than a mutual fund. This allows investors to noticeably diversify their portfolios with much less capital. Because of these benefits, ETFs have been gaining in popularity. At the end of 2015, there were nearly 1,600 ETFs in the United States with combined assets of $2.1 trillion. Each year more and more funds are flowing into ETFs but they are still far behind mutual funds which hold more than $16 trillion.

While ETFs are rising in popularity, they aren't a magic investment that will allow you a free ride. As explained, most ETFs are not actively managed which means it is up to the individual investor to adjust the percentage held in one ETF or another. It is up to you to recognize when an ETF's holdings are becoming overvalued, to know when to reposition the assets, and what to purchase next.

Passive vs. active

For decades, the investment world has debated which of the two basic approaches to investing produces the best returns: Active or Passive.

In the corner for active trading are those that argue that hand-picking investments can generate returns that exceed the benchmark. They argue that through analysis and research, higher returns could be generated by exchanging holdings while also lowering the overall risk of the investment. But because active management is more expensive, the returns must not only beat the index they must be high enough to cover the extra costs.

In the other corner are those that argue using low cost, passively managed funds produces better results. Passive funds seek to mirror the performance of an index while keeping fees and transaction costs at a minimum. They argue that remaining invested at all times—meaning you capture all the upside when the market is up and all the downside when the market drops—results in better overall returns. But remember, the goal of the passive funds is to directly follow the market rather than to try to beat it.

The data shows that although actively managed funds can beat the market, the majority do not. While there are top-rated fund managers that can get exceptional results, even these superstars can have bad years, and few are able to significantly beat the markets on a consistent basis. Keep in mind that actively managed funds (i.e. mutual funds) are handicapped because they must keep 80% invested in assets specific to the fund description. The inability to diversify more or move to low risk options during high volatility limits the ability of managed funds to consistently outperform the market.

% of Funds to Outperform the Benchmark

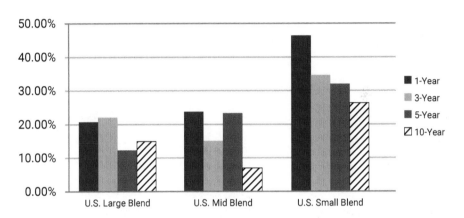

Source: Morningstar: Data and calculations 6/30/16

Tactical money management

As we've already discussed, passively or actively managed funds are no longer the only options for investing your money. Because of the rise of ETFs, other management strategies have been developed that have demonstrated the ability to produce better-than-market returns.

Tactical management has evolved as a new way to invest. There are many different methods of tactical management, but the basic idea to actively manage ETFs is to adjust your asset allocations in order to increase returns, reduce risk, or both. Tactical management allows the investor to move out of asset classes that are showing signs of stress or overvaluation, and reposition the investments in classes that are growing or undervalued. Because tactical management is done through ETFs and not mutual funds, it allows the manager complete flexibility in the make-up of the portfolio.

Let's take real estate for example. From 2007 to 2009 real estate was one of the worst assets to be holding. Losses exceeded 50% on many funds and exposure to this asset class inside your portfolio would have had devastating results. Using a tactical management strategy all real estate holdings could have been sold off the moment indicators started signaling weakness.

There are a myriad of different techniques—from rebalancing your portfolio to stay at certain asset allocation percentages, to using probabilities, momentum, or indicators in the market as signals to know when it's time to change your allocations—to tactically manage your ETFs. But the point is that all of these methods, each with their own pros and cons, are available because of the agile nature of ETFs.

Picking the right strategy

Have you ever played an empire-building board game like *Monopoly*? The object of the game is to build your empire by amassing real estate holdings and then developing those properties to grow their earning potential. When you begin the game you usually have a certain strategy in mind for how and when you want to invest. For example, I liked acquiring all of the "yellow" properties while my brother loved creating a real estate empire in the "low priced" district. At the end of the day regardless of the initial plan, you are always at the mercy of the dice. Depending on the numbers you (or your opponents) roll on the dice, you may have to try a couple different strategies or adjust your plans throughout the game.

That is not unlike building your investment portfolio, except, you know, now it's with your actual hard-earned dollars at stake. But on a fundamental level, you still cannot control the role of the dice or the fluctuations of the market, and so often multiple strategies will need to be employed in order to reach your goals and simultaneously protect your nest egg.

Evaluate all of your security investments with the value proposition in mind: What was my return? How much risk did I take? And what did it cost me in fees and taxes? As you weigh these questions against your goals and objectives, you can better decide which strategies are best for your hard-earned money. As we continue through the book we will be discussing other keys to factor into these investment decisions that will allow you to achieve success in retirement.

CHAPTER 7

ANNUITIES

"Get your facts first, and then you can distort them as much as you please."
— Mark Twain

I had a potential client that had saved up a substantial retirement portfolio in various accounts but was spending very little of it because his Social Security benefits covered 80% of his income needs. Despite having over a million dollars in savings, I discovered in our early planning, that he was actually scared to spend any of it because his investments were fairly risky. The volatility of his accounts made him worry about spending anything, especially in years when the markets were down. As we discussed his investments, I showed him some changes we could make that would reduce his risk and allow him to worry less about his accounts.

When we finished he was frankly shocked. He said, "Aren't you going to try to sell me an annuity?" I explained that he had no need for an annuity because most of his income needs were already covered by his Social Security benefits and his investments would allow him to comfortably withdraw the rest of his income needs from his IRAs. There was no need for an annuity in his financial plan, but that had not prevented lots of people from trying to sell him one.

The word "annuity" elicits a fairly wide range of reactions from investors. Often when I meet with new clients and mention the word "annuity," they act like I just called their grandchild "ugly." The reaction is immediate and instinctive. Unfortunately, there is so much misinformation and inaccuracy surrounding annuities that some people won't even consider them as an option for their retirement plan, even when it might be one of their best choices.

Now, I'll be the first to admit that annuities have been given a "black eye" over the years and in a lot of cases it's justified. For years, annuities have been aggressively pitched by Wall Street brokers or overzealous insurance agents. If you are approaching retirement you can attest to the fact that your mailbox is full of invitations to "free steak dinners." We all know there's no such thing as a "free steak dinner" and what you're likely signing up for is a high pressure pitch to buy an annuity. These high pressure tactics have been going on for years and the approach has left a bad taste in investors' mouths. (And I'm not just talking about the steak.)

The thing is, not all annuities are good, but at the same time, not all of them are bad. Understanding the different kinds of annuities, their features and benefits, and where they can fit into a retirement plan is an important step in navigating the new retirement. Like any other investment, the decision to buy an annuity should be made for a specific reason and as part of a larger financial plan.

Types of annuities

The standard definition of an annuity is a financial product that pays out a steady amount of income over a specified period of time, but this over-simplified definition is undergoing changes as the design of annuities are changing to meet the needs of how people are retiring today.

All annuities are not the same and there are key differences in the way they are designed.

Single Premium Immediate Annuity (SPIA)

SPIAs are actually the most common types of annuities. In fact, most pensions are in reality an SPIA. An SPIA is used to generate a guaranteed income stream that will continue for the life of the annuitant or for a specified period of time.

It is designed to generate the most income possible, but once triggered, you can no longer withdraw a lump sum. Because the lump sum is forfeited, it is very uncommon for someone to invest their retirement account into this type of annuity but is most commonly used for structured settlements.

Fixed Annuity

A fixed annuity* is offered by an insurance company and is similar to certificate of deposits (CDs) provided by your local bank. Like a CD, they pay a guaranteed interest rate for a specified period of time. At the end of the term, you can withdraw 100% of the amount invested and the accrued interest with no penalty. Generally, the term of a fixed annuity is longer than a CD but the positive trade-off is that the annuity's fixed interest rate is often much better.

---

* Fixed Annuities are long term insurance contracts and there is a surrender charge imposed generally during the first 5 to 7 years that you own the annuity contract. Withdrawals prior to age 59-1/2 may result in a 10% IRS tax penalty, in addition to any ordinary income tax. Any guarantees of the annuity are backed by the financial strength of the underlying insurance company.

Variable Annuity (VA)

If you have purchased an annuity in the past, you likely owned a variable annuity.* VAs are the main culprit in giving annuities a bad reputation. Due to investment risk and high fees, many investors felt they were sold a bill of goods. A variable annuity is actually a security and funds are invested in mutual funds or ETFs, which means you can lose money depending on the investments that are chosen.

If the risk wasn't bad enough, variable annuities are also notorious for fees stacked on top of fees. While the funds inside the VA have the same types of fees that you find in most mutual funds, VAs also charge fees for administrative costs, mortality and expense risk, and riders. It is not

---

* Please consider the investment objectives, risks, charges, and expenses carefully before investing in Variable Annuities. The prospectus, which contains this and other information about the variable annuity contract and the underlying investment options, can be obtained from the insurance company or your financial professional. Be sure to read the prospectus carefully before deciding whether to invest.

The investment return and principal value of the variable annuity investment options are not guaranteed. Variable annuity sub-accounts fluctuate with changes in market conditions. The principal may be worth more or less than the original amount invested when the annuity is surrendered.

uncommon once all of the fees are added up to be paying over 3% annually. With all of the fees dragging the performance of the account down, it's no wonder people have such strong emotions when they hear the word "annuity."

Fixed Index Annuity (FIA)

The newest and fastest growing type of annuity is the fixed indexed annuity.* FIAs allow you to receive interest based on the performance of an index but if the index goes down your principal is protected from loss. In other words, your account can grow based on the performance of the index but won't suffer a loss if the index heads into negative territory. This is a huge reduction in risk and something to consider in relation to your value proposition.

---

* Fixed indexed annuities are insurance contracts that, depending on the contract, may offer a guaranteed annual interest rate and some participation growth, if any, of a stock market index. Such contracts have substantial variation in terms, costs of guarantees and features and may cap participation or returns in significant ways. Any guarantees offered are backed by the financial strength of the insurance company. Surrender charges apply if not held to the end of the term. Withdrawals are taxed as ordinary income and, if taken prior to 59 ½, a 10% federal tax penalty can be assessed. Investors are cautioned to carefully review an indexed annuity for its features, costs, risks, and how the variables are calculated.

FIAs use various crediting strategies to determine how much interest you receive in a given year. The most common crediting methods are as follows:

Cap

A "cap" is the maximum interest that can be credited during a specific term. The cap will limit the amount credited if the index return exceeds the cap. For example, if the annual cap on an annuity is 4% and the index produces a return of 9% only the cap amount of 4% will be credited to the account. If the index produces a return of 3%, the account would be credited with the entire 3% since it is below the cap. The cap can be changed at the beginning of each term and caps are generally set lower when interest rates are low.

Participation Rate

Some annuities use a participation rate or percentage to determine how much interest is credited to the account. For example, if the index increased by 10% and the participation rate was 75%, the account would be credited 7.5%.

Fee or Spread

Another method for crediting interest is the use of a fee or spread. This works similar to a mutual fund where the index return is reduced by the set fee or spread. For example, if the index produced a 7% return and the fee or spread was 2%, then the amount credited to the account would be 5%.

The difference between a fee and a spread is that fees are always subtracted, while a spread is only subtracted when the returns are positive. A spread would not be deducted in years of negative returns and the account value would remain unchanged.

The most common misconception

The most common misconception that exists about annuities is the belief that once you put money into an annuity, you will never have access to it again. Many people incorrectly believe that if they pass away with money still in their annuity account that the insurance company will keep all of their hard-earned money, laughing all the way to the bank. This is absolutely untrue but I can't tell you how many people have come in to my office believing this is how annuities work.

The only annuity where you forfeit the rights to the lump sum is the SPIA. All other annuities allow the lump sum to be withdrawn, including all accrued interest, at the end of the contract.

Now this doesn't mean that there aren't restrictions on when and how much can be withdrawn.

Because of the guarantees provided in the annuity contract, the insurance company will restrict the amount that can be withdrawn during something called the surrender period. Surrender periods can range from 6 to 20 years but are typically 8 to 12 years long. During the surrender period, a free withdrawal amount, typically 5-10% annually can be withdrawn without penalty. A fee or charge would be deducted from the amount withdrawn for any amount above the allowed amount.

There are special exceptions where the surrender penalty is waived and 100% of the account can be withdrawn with no charge. These exceptions include: being diagnosed with a terminal illness, being confined to a nursing home, or at death.

Because annuities are not as liquid as other investments it is very important to maintain a proper balance in the type of investments that make up your portfolio. As with most things, the key is balance. Putting too much into one company or allocation is never a good idea and the same applies to annuities. The most common reason surrender charges come into play is too much was put into the annuities in the beginning and not enough was left liquid and available.

Tax rules for annuities

One advantage annuities provide is tax-deferred growth. Tax deferral means postponing the payment of taxes on the gains until the funds are withdrawn from the account. In the meantime, you continue to make money on the money that would have otherwise been paid to Uncle Sam. Over time this means more money in your pocket. For example, deferring the taxes on a $100,000 investment with annual growth of 8% results in additional interest earnings of $27,070. The drawback to this tax deferral is that the growth is taxed at ordinary income tax rates and not at the capital gains tax rate. The various tax rates now and in the future will determine the overall potential tax benefit.

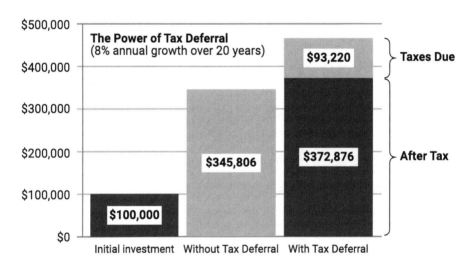

*Assumed tax rate of 20%

Why annuities

So, you're probably wondering which annuity should be used and when. Because each type of annuity has different features and drawbacks, it's important to determine your goals and objectives as part of a comprehensive retirement plan.

	ANNUITY TYPE			
	SPIA	FIXED	FIXED INDEXED	VARIABLE
RATE OF RETURN	Rate determines monthly payout	Locked-in, guaranteed fixed rate	Upside potential return limited by crediting strategy	Return based on performance of chosen sub-accounts
PRINCIPAL PROTECTION	N/A	YES	YES	NO
TAX-DEFERRAL	Distributed interest is taxable	YES	YES	YES
LIFETIME INCOME	YES	YES	YES	YES
LUMP SUM AVAILABLE	NO	YES	YES	YES
WHO WOULD BENEFIT	Someone seeking immediate monthly income	Someone seeking a fixed rate; rate is usually higher than a CD	Someone seeking for more potential upside while still protecting principal	Someone willing to take market risk but wants tax deferral

As noted above, all annuities have the ability to provide a lifetime income. In fact, producing income is where annuities really shine because of guarantees, high payout ratios, and optional riders. This is one of the reasons that they have grown in popularity over the past decade as more and more people retire without a pension. In Chapter 13, we will go into detail on how annuities can be used to maximize income during retirement and ensure you don't outlive your money.

KEYS TO NAVIGATION

With a good appreciation of the new retirement landscape, we are now ready to learn and understand the keys that will help you navigate it successfully. In the following chapters we will talk about the principles of diversification and risk mitigation, the importance of stage of life investing and tax efficiency, avoiding losses and reducing or eliminating their impact on your portfolio, as well as understanding the true impact of fees on your account balances and increasing your retirement income efficiency.

These keys are designed to help you avoid the pitfalls and mistakes that can threaten the security of your retirement, decrease your worry and anxiety, and empower you to achieve and realize your retirement dreams.

When I was a teenager we went on a family trip, but two of my brothers had to work and planned to meet up with us a day later. They left late at night after work, and decided that one of them would drive for a few hours while the other one slept.

The plan was to trade places when they got to Flagstaff, 2.5 hours north of Phoenix. When my brother Jared woke up two and a half hours later, expecting to be in the mountains of Flagstaff, he was shocked to see the bright city lights and signage of Phoenix. My brother Jacob had driven in circles around the Phoenix metro for two and half hours, unable to figure out which freeway would take him north—driving the car, certainly, but not actually going anywhere.

Jared was *not* happy with their lack of progress and asked in complete aggravation, "Why didn't you wake me up?" Jake replied that for a long time he didn't know he was lost and by the time he realized it he was too embarrassed to ask and just hoped he'd figure it out.

Your retirement plan needs to work. It needs to actually take you somewhere, rather than just look like it's doing something when it's really only going around in circles. Too many times, our retirement strategies counteract each other and we shuffle around without making any real progress or reaching our true goals. Worse yet, we often don't even know we aren't getting anywhere and feel inadequate and stupid when we discover it. The keys in the next six chapters can help you clearly define your objectives, align your strategies with your goals, give you confidence to seek out the right help, and navigate your way to a successful retirement.

CHAPTER 8

KEY #1: DIVERSIFICATION VS. CORRELATION

"It's OK to have your eggs in one basket as long as you control what happens to that basket."
— **Elon Musk**

Imagine a football team where all 11 players on the field were quarterbacks. Who would protect the quarterback? Who would catch the ball? Who would hike it or kick it? Having both Joe Montana and Tom Brady on your team may seem like a dream, but if Brady was running routes and Joe was throwing to him, I'm guessing the results wouldn't be very pretty. (Besides we all know the best quarterback ever was Danny White—see Chapter One—but the analogy still works.) You could have the best eleven quarterbacks who ever played on the field, but because the team lacks the other specialties—players with different skills, abilities, and expertise—your All-Star team of quarterbacks wouldn't stand a chance. In other words, a championship team needs diversification—each player doing his job, making every other player better at their own jobs.

Your portfolio works the same way. It can't be competitive if all the investments are doing the same job—that leaves holes and deficits in your protection and your performance. We need to have a diversified investment strategy.* It's one of those common investment buzzwords we all know we should be doing. Unfortunately, more often than not, the average portfolio is not as diversified as it should be.

People come into our office already knowing they need to be diversified. They pull out their statements and point out the variety of descriptions their portfolio contains: value, growth, small-cap, international funds, and then sit back with a satisfied look on their faces thinking they already have this strategy mastered. The problem is that diversification is more than assembling a bunch of separate funds or holdings.

---

* Diversification does not guarantee a profit or protect against a loss in a declining market. It is a method used to help manage investment risk.

Correlation is key

One of the most common problems I see when meeting with a new client is that although their portfolios have "lots of different funds," the funds are moving up and down in tandem. In the investment world, this phenomenon is known as correlation.

Correlation determines how closely related the movements of one holding are to the various other holdings in a portfolio. In other words, as one fund rises or falls, how much does another fund in the same portfolio move in the same or opposite direction. Remember, you can't have a team of all quarterbacks and be successful. You need different kinds of players to reach your goals. You need a lineman who will push forward and block the defensive end, while your quarterback stands in the pocket and looks for the wide receiver, who is wide open downfield.

While a portfolio should contain several different kinds of funds, the key is understanding how correlated they are. If all the funds move up or down together, they are highly correlated, which in turn means they are not very diversified. They are all quarterbacks. Even though they appear to be unique funds, if they *behave the same* in both the good and bad times, you are essentially invested in one fund.

Understanding correlation is quite simple. If a fund exactly mirrors another fund it would have a correlation of 1.0, meaning they move in tandem at all times. On the flip side, a correlation of -1.0 would tell you that the two funds move exactly opposite at all times. While it is virtually impossible to find an investment with perfect correlations of 1.0 or -1.0, any fund that is not perfectly correlated with another provides some level of diversification.

The goal of diversification is to build a portfolio made up of holdings with a low correlation to each other. This means all the holdings will not move in tandem which is especially important when the market is declining.

Because we can't always pick the right stock or "control what happens to our basket" once it enters the market, we need to diversify to make sure we aren't "all in" on a loser. If your entire basket is too closely correlated, what happens to one egg is likely to happen to all of them.

Globalization and diversification

Keep in mind that diversification is getting more and more difficult because our global economy is becoming more and more correlated. Not long ago, you could buy an international investment that had a very low correlation to your domestic holdings. Unfortunately, the correlation between international and domestic stocks has steadily risen due to the globalization of economies around the world and the expansion of multinational companies. As a result, today the news out of China or Europe can cause some pretty serious shockwaves in the US stock market.

In 1997, the correlation between the S&P 500 and the MSCI EAFE (International) Index was .45. Over the past twenty years the correlation has risen significantly to .90. As the correlation has increased, these seemingly "diversified" assets are providing less and less diversification benefits.

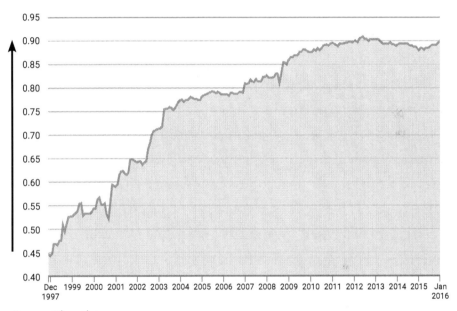

Source: Bloomberg

Correlation of S&P 500 to the MSCI EAFE Index

Stock intersection

Another thing to keep in mind when you are examining your diversification is that many different funds invest in the exact same stocks; so when you invest in multiple funds, it is likely that you are holding the exact same stock many times over.

This is known as stock intersection or fund overlap. For example, Apple stock is likely to be held within several different funds within your portfolio. When this happens, the ups and downs of this one stock, will impact the performance of your whole portfolio. The more stock intersection your portfolio has, clearly the less diversified you are, regardless of fund name or category.

Even the indices—like the Dow Jones, Nasdaq, and S&P 500—which we use to measure the overall performance of the stock market are not as diversified as most people believe.

The S&P 500, for example, contains 500 different stocks, which gives the appearance of being very diversified, but in reality it is not as diversified as you would think. The S&P 500 is market-value-weighted, meaning that the stocks of larger companies have more influence on the overall performance—they carry more weight. So much so that nearly half of the total market capitalization of this 500-stock index comes from just 50 of its stocks. For example, Apple, by market cap, is the largest stock in the S&P 500 index. Its weight is currently almost twice that of the next two largest stocks, Microsoft and Exxon Mobil, and carries 197 times the weight of the smallest stock in the index, Diamond Offshore Drilling. What that means is that even though you are technically invested in 500 different stocks (diversified!), the fate and performance of the index is heavily tied to the fates of just a few of those (not diversified!).

Theory vs. reality

The trouble is that diversification in theory is awesome and wise and obvious, but putting it into practice in the real world is a whole different story. There are always going to be those moments where you second guess the diversification strategy...because look how much money you could have made if you had gone "all in" in that other sector of your portfolio! What were you thinking?

Diversification with low correlation by definition means that when some stocks go up, others are going to flat line or (gasp!) decline. No one sets out in the market to decline. You're a winner, after all. You and Danny White. What are you doing in asset classes that are performing badly?

Diversification is like eating right. It makes sense, you know it's good for you, you know you'll be happier with the results in the long run, but in the short term it seems like every one is having fun without you. You're trading your french fries for a side of broccoli and while it makes sense and you can stand it for a while, eventually you give in and start ordering the french fries and 100% pure US stocks. What could go wrong?

Then it's 2008, your cholesterol is out of control, you have a massive coronary, and you promise to give broccoli another try. Just remember that the alternative to diversification is to just always, always pick the investments that are going up. If you can do that with every investment, every day, then you never need to diversify. And if you can always pick the right stock, why not just buy the winning lottery ticket while you're at it.

A cautionary tale

I have a really good friend who began to invest heavily in real estate back in 2005. As you may remember, this was during the great real estate boom where just about anyone could make money in real estate and just about everyone was trying to. For a couple of years, things were great. He bought and sold houses and acquired some land that he then split into lots and sold off. Everything he touched turned to gold and he was making money hand over fist.

But then 2007 rolled around and along with it came the mortgage-backed securities crisis and subsequent real estate recession. My friend went from being a real estate mogul raking in piles of money to, seemingly overnight, wondering if they were going to be able to keep their house. For two years his undiversified bet on real estate paid off handsomely, but one bad year wiped out everything. The lack of diversification caught up to him.

Eventually, it catches up to everyone. Because markets change, crashes happen, bubbles burst, winning assets decline. That is certain. What is less certain is predicting exactly when it's going to happen. In the blink of an eye going "all in" can wipe out everything, everything you've worked so hard to earn and to save. Diversification spreads out this risk and allows you to temper and cushion those undesirable outcomes, to soften the blow, and protect your hard-earned money.

CHAPTER 9

KEY #2: STAGE OF LIFE INVESTING

*"If you have trouble imagining
a 20% loss in the stock market,
you shouldn't be in stocks."*
— John Bogle, Founder of Vanguard

In our retirement workshops I will usually ask the room, "How many of you were concerned about your retirement portfolios and their performance when you were in your thirties?" I usually only get a couple of people that raise their hands (and they are the type that were also concerned at age 10 and have the spreadsheets to prove it). I will then ask the class, "How many of you watch your accounts today?" Almost all of the hands shoot up, from the teacher to the executive; everyone becomes more interested in their retirement accounts the closer they get to those golden years. While some people might be paying more attention because the accounts are now worth more, the main reason they are closely watching them is because as they approach retirement the reality of actually needing those funds is starting to hit.

Have you ever filled out a risk assessment to determine your investor risk profile? Through a series of questions, designed to gauge your risk tolerance, expectations, and objectives in investing, a portfolio with a certain level of risk can be recommended. One of the most important factors in this risk assessment is the time horizon of the investment. The two main questions are: How long will it be before you will need to start using funds from the account? And how long do you want those funds to last?

Time has a way of changing our perspective and priorities. What we need or what our priorities are depends on the stage of life we are in. When discussing this concept with our clients we break it down into three stages of investing that each have their own goals and objectives which are unique to that stage of life. The three stages of life as it relates to investing are: accumulation, preservation, and distribution.

Accumulation

The *accumulation phase* starts in your 20s and continues through your early to mid-50s. In this phase you are finishing school, advancing in your career, getting married, and starting a family. At the beginning of this phase most people are paying for larger expenses and purchases (i.e. education and mortgages) and very little money is allocated to retirement accounts and other long-term investments. Once you have settled into your career and life, people start socking away money into various investments accounts—IRAs, 401(k)s, etc.

Because time is on your side, most investors choose long-term investments where they can take more risk and get better returns. For the most part the ups and downs of the market go largely unnoticed as you continue to diligently add money to your accounts each month. During the accumulation phase, you have a general idea of how much you should save up to be able to retire, but because it is so far out in the future you're not too worried about where you're at and how you are tracking.

When someone hits their 50s and approaches the end of the accumulation phase, we start seeing a change. The amount they have saved up starts becoming a major focus and preparing for retirement becomes a priority.

Preservation

About five years before someone is planning to retire, they enter what we call the *preservation phase*. This is where the focus starts to shift from trying to double and triple the money in your account to making sure you don't lose it just before you want to retire. It is critical that the primary investment objective shift from growth to safety prior to retirement so that a major market correction doesn't delay or cancel your retirement plans. The goal of the preservation phase will overlap the final phase (distribution), as preservation is also a critical component of the distribution phase.

Distribution

As you enter retirement you are now faced with the task of replacing your paycheck. For some who retire with pensions and Social Security, the *distribution phase* can be pushed out for a few years, but for many, the distribution phase begins on Day 1 of retirement. During the distribution phase you must decide how much to withdraw from your investments while still making sure your money lasts as long as you do. Because losses and withdrawals go together about as well as oil and water (we will talk about this in detail in Chapter 10), following the investment strategies established during the preservation stage become more and more critical. Because your goal is making sure you have money as long as you are alive, your investments should be allocated towards strategies that promote stability and sustainability.

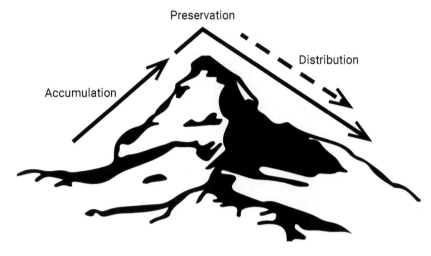

STAGE OF LIFE INVESTING

Why stage of life investing is so important

The reason stage of life investing is so important is because the volatility of the same investment can vary greatly when evaluated over different time periods. In other words, just because an investment did well over a long period of time does not mean that it will perform well over shorter periods of time. Take the Dow Jones index for example. If you look at the Dow's performance over 35-year periods, taking day-by-day snapshots, the worst 35-year period you can find still produced an average return of 6.1%, a return most of us would be pretty comfortable with during retirement. But if you take the same index and look at shorter time periods, the volatility and average return is dramatically different.

Time Period	Worst Return During Time Period (Dow Jones)
1 Year	-52.7%
5 Years	-16.4%
10 Years	-1.3%
20 Years	2.5%
35 Years	6.1%

While you are in the accumulation phase, time is on your side, which generally results in more consistent and predictable returns over the long haul. But when you shorten the time period of that same investment the returns will become more volatile and unpredictable, jeopardizing the success of your retirement plan.

Target date funds

This realization that investment strategies should change as your stage of life changes, has led to a rise in a new kind of mutual fund: the "target-date fund." The basic idea behind these funds is that, as you approach retirement, the makeup and composition of the fund is gradually adjusted to become more conservative. This gradual adjustment to a more conservative allocation is known as a "glide path" and, in theory, reduces the risk of the portfolio. If you take the time to look at the investment options in your 401(k) plan, you will likely notice at least of few of these target-date funds (TDFs), also known as "lifecycle funds." Over the past decade, the amount of money invested in TDFs has exploded with just under $800 billion being invested so far.

Why such rapid growth?

The rise of target-date funds can be traced back to the Pension Protection Act of 2006, which allowed the Department of Labor to develop approved "default options" for investing retirement funds. As part of this legislation, if an employer chooses one of these approved options and makes it the default option for employer and employee contributions, the employers cannot be held liable. In other words, if a company adds TDFs as one of the options within their plan and makes them the default option for future contributions, the company cannot be held liable for poor performance in the fund.

As a result, employers began to automatically enroll new employees into 401(k)s and choose TDFs as the default option—auto-investing in the TDF unless the employee actively chose another option. As several studies have shown, most people will make no changes to the default option selected when their account is initially set up, and so the money directed toward target-date funds has begun to pile up.

Misconceptions and dangers

Unfortunately, as more and more money has been directed towards target-date funds, the misconception that these funds are a "set-it-and-forget-it" investment option has increased. The Securities and Exchange Commission (Investor Testing Report, 2012) conducted a survey that revealed some startling misconceptions about target-date funds. Only 30% of respondents were able to identify the correct meaning of the year in the fund's name and 64% incorrectly believed the TDF would provide a guaranteed income stream in retirement, regardless of market performance. Not surprisingly, 54% of respondents assumed that two different funds with the same year in their name would have the same mix of stocks and bonds at the specified target date, which may seem like a reasonable assumption, but is also incorrect.

In the survey, respondents revealed that the top reason for choosing TDFs was because "it seems like a safe investment for retirement." Many have assumed the "glide path" is automatically going to provide a safe landing for their retirement funds, but the crash of 2008 proved this perception to be devastatingly incorrect.

Take, for example, target-date funds with a date of 2010. In 2008, only 15 months before the target retirement date, you might assume these funds would be conservatively allocated. Unfortunately, investors standing at retirement's doorstep suffered average losses of nearly -24% with losses ranging between -17% and -41%. A closer look at what caused these losses revealed that the average fund had more than 50% still invested in stocks—only 15 months before the target date!—when the market plummeted.

Executing the plan

Have you ever watched Olympic track and field events? After the races, broadcasters often interview the runners and ask them how they felt about their race. Most of the time, the athletes focus their comments on their plan for the race and how successful they felt they were in executing that plan.

As part of the preparation for race day, runners and coaches make a race strategy; they map the race, lap by lap, turn by turn, determining ahead of time where they will push the pace, where they will hold steady despite what other runners are doing around them, and where they will break out and try to take the lead. These plans include contingencies for when a race is run "fast" or "slow" and other variables they can't control.

After the races, they compare their performance with the plan, analyzing how they executed the plan despite the pressures and anxieties and unknowns of race day. This is how they measure their success: Did I stick to the plan? Did I execute *my* race? Over and over I've heard racers say, "I felt really good. I ran it the way I wanted to. When so-and-so broke ahead, I didn't panic, I stuck to the plan."

Stage of life retirement planning requires the same kind of discipline and preparation. There are different strategies for each stage of the race. If you employ the wrong tactic in the wrong phase, you won't be as successful and even run the risk of not being able to finish. If you simply "set-it-and-forget-it" you won't be able to respond to unexpected "race day" challenges. You need a comprehensive investment strategy that can help you be disciplined and wise during every stage of life, adapt to the changing conditions of the current market, and give you the confidence to stick with the plan.

CHAPTER 10

KEY #3: DON'T LOSE IT IN THE FIRST PLACE

"Rule No.1: Never lose money. Rule No.2: Never forget rule No.1."
— **Warren Buffett**

After I have met with a client for the first time, one of the things I do to prepare for our next appointment is conduct a portfolio analysis so we can discuss the strengths and vulnerabilities of their investments. While some portfolios are being managed properly, all too often I find that people in retirement or right on its doorstep are taking way too much risk. Sadly, this comes as a shock to many of them as well. Before we talk about the results, I will often ask how they would describe their portfolio. The most common response goes something like, "Well, I think it's pretty balanced. I told my guy that I didn't want to be too risky." As we then begin reviewing the results of the analysis, they immediately realize how much risk they were actually taking and the potential issues that could impact their nest egg.

Too many people think that to grow their money, they have to take risks. This is simply not the case. Now, you can't just hide your money under your mattress and expect it to last as long as you do. But on the flip side, it's often unnecessary risk that causes people to fail in retirement and run out of money.

We tell our clients, "Our #1 job is to protect your money. Our #2 job is to grow it." A successful retirement is built on protecting your nest egg. If we can just avoid the big losses, we don't need double digit returns and your money will still last forever.

The bottom line is: The losses in your portfolio will have a much greater impact than any of your gains.

The impact of losses

The impact of losses on a portfolio cannot be overstated. Really, you are losing twice. First, you lose the money you have invested or grown over time, and then going forward you now have less money to invest, which makes all future gains less than what they would have been. Let's say you invest $10,000 and your investment goes down by 30%. You now have $7,000. The next year the investment goes up by 30%. Fine, you say, I broke even. But you'd be wrong. 30% of $7,000 only gives you $9,100. You would actually need a 43% return just to break even.

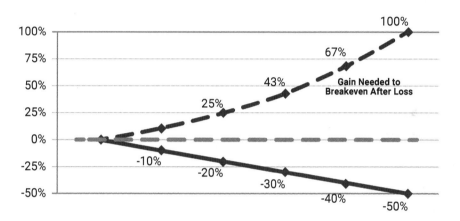

During the "Great Recession," the S&P 500 dropped 56.8% from its peak on October 9, 2007 to the bottom on March 9, 2009. To get back to pre-crash numbers, the S&P 500 needed an astounding 131% return, which fortunately only took four years. While four years seems like a long time, it was actually a very quick recovery. For example, when the NASDAQ index plummeted when the dot-com bubble burst back in 2001, it took 14 years for that index to return to pre-crash numbers.

And that's only part of the true loss picture. If we're being honest, when you have a loss, you're really losing three times because you also lose the time in the market at your pre-loss value.

It took four years to return to pre-crash numbers, but that means you also lost four years of growth, four years where you were not making money on that money, four years where those dollars were just fighting to get back to where they were. Those people who thought they would be ready to retire by 2013, instead found themselves exactly where they were five or six years earlier and they could only thank their lucky stars that it wasn't worse.

As if that wasn't bad enough, how would your accounts look if you were already in retirement and drawing money from your nest egg during this downturn? Would you have been able to afford to leave your money untouched while the market recovered? For many, the answer to this question is "No." So, what does that mean for your future retirement? Will you be able to recover from the next downturn in the market or will it put your retirement in jeopardy? Well, that depends on something called the "sequence of returns."

Sequence of returns

Sequence of returns is one of the most important concepts to understand and may be the most important factor in determining how long your assets last during retirement. Yes, you heard me right. The sequence (or the order) of your returns can be more important than the average rate of return on your investment.

There are two rules that govern how your money accumulates and grows. One rule applies while you are accumulating and building your nest egg. The other rule is applied while you are spending from that nest egg. The problem is that nobody tells you that the rules have changed. As a result, many people don't even realize things are different until it is often too late.

So, what are the two rules?

Rule #1: The sequence (or order) of returns has no impact on your final account value while you are growing your money.

Rule #2: Once you begin taking withdrawals, the sequence (or order) of positive and negative returns will significantly change the value of the account.

When you are in the accumulation phase (not withdrawing money), the order or timing of the returns has no impact whatsoever on your final account balance. On the other hand, when you begin taking money from your accounts, it is all about timing. More specifically, it's about the timing of the negative returns. Negative returns in the first few years after you start withdrawing funds will cause you to deplete your account balance at a much greater rate than if you received those negative returns at the end of the investment. Consider the following charts:

Sequence of Returns
During Accumulation Period

Deposit: $100,000
Assumptions: 10 years, No withdrawals

EXAMPLE A

Year	Return	Gain/Loss	Ending Value
1	-30%	-$30,000	$70,000
2	-20%	-$14,000	$56,000
3	10%	$5,600	$61,600
4	10%	$6,160	$67,760
5	10%	$6,776	$74,536
6	10%	$7,454	$81,990
7	10%	$8,199	$90,189
8	10%	$9,019	$99,208
9	20%	$19,841	$119,049
10	30%	$35,715	**$154,764**

EXAMPLE B *(Returns are inverse of Ex. A)*

Year	Return	Gain/Loss	Ending Value
1	30%	$30,000	$130,000
2	20%	$26,000	$156,000
3	10%	$15,600	$171,600
4	10%	$17,160	$188,760
5	10%	$18,776	$207,636
6	10%	$20,764	$228,400
7	10%	$22,840	$251,240
8	10%	$25,124	$276,364
9	-20%	-$55,273	$221,091
10	-30%	-$66,327	**$154,764**

In the illustration, both examples generate the same average return over a ten year period. The only difference is that Example A experiences losses at the beginning of the investment while the losses come at the end of the investment in Example B. It is true that the ending values are dramatically different year over year but when we get to the end of the ten years both investments have identical account balances.

Whether your losses happened in year 1 and 2, or year 9 and 10, you end up with the same account balance of $154,764. The ending values in each scenario are identical which proves Rule #1.

Now look at the difference in the results if we are in a distribution phase. In the following example, you are still making an initial investment of $100,000, but now you are also taking out $6,000 a year to supplement your income.

Sequence of Returns
While taking withdrawals

Deposit: $100,000
Assumptions: 10 years, $6,000/yr. withdrawal

EXAMPLE A

Year	Return	Beginning Value	Withdrawal	Ending Value
		$100,000		
1	-30%	$70,000	-$6,000	$64,000
2	-20%	$51,200	-$6,000	$45,200
3	10%	$49,720	-$6,000	$43,720
4	10%	$48,092	-$6,000	$42,092
5	10%	$46,301	-$6,000	$70,301
6	10%	$44,331	-$6,000	$38,331
7	10%	$42,164	-$6,000	$36,164
8	10%	$39,781	-$6,000	$33,781
9	20%	$40,537	-$6,000	$34,537
10	30%	$44,898	-$6,000	**$38,898**

EXAMPLE B *(Returns are inverse of Ex. A)*

Year	Return	Beginning Value	Withdrawal	Ending Value
		$100,000		
1	30%	$130,000	-$6,000	$124,000
2	20%	$148,800	-$6,000	$142,800
3	10%	$157,080	-$6,000	$151,080
4	10%	$166,188	-$6,000	$160,188
5	10%	$176,207	-$6,000	$170,207
6	10%	$187,227	-$6,000	$181,227
7	10%	$199,350	-$6,000	$193,350
8	10%	$212,685	-$6,000	$206,685
9	-20%	$165,348	-$6,000	$159,348
10	-30%	$111,544	-$6,000	**$105,544**

In Example A, the negative returns happen in the first two years of the investment, whereas in Example B you have the same negative returns but they happen at the end of the investment period. As you can clearly see, the timing of negative returns during the distribution phase made a huge difference ($66,646) in the ending values of the two investments. Notice that even though both examples had the same *average* return, the *actual* account balances are significantly different! In Example A you are at risk of running out of money while in Example B you actually have more money than what you started with even after ten years of withdrawals.

The sequence of returns matters

For years, financial advisors told their clients they could safely withdraw 4% from their investment accounts and they would never run out of money. Advisors would run an illustration, pick a hypothetical rate of return, show withdrawals coming out each year, with money left over. What could go wrong?

The problem is that there is a difference between *average* returns and *actual* returns because the markets don't produce a steady average return year over year. Every market year is different—some years have gains and others have losses. Over time you receive an "average rate of return," but those averages can't protect you from the significant impact of *actual* losses at the start of the withdrawal period.

Over the past fifteen years, we have seen the markets move up and down with considerable volatility, and that volatility can have a dramatic impact on the balance of your portfolio in terms of sequence of returns. For example, if you invested $100,000 in the S&P 500 and withdrew 4% each year from the year 2000 to 2010, because of the effect of sequence of returns you would have just over $30,000 left in your account. If that trend continued, within just a few short years your account would be completely exhausted.

In the real world, sequence of returns matters. If an advisor fails to factor sequence of returns into your plan, they are essentially crossing their fingers and hoping that the returns line up in the perfect order so the money is there when you need it. But if they are wrong, you're the one looking for a part-time job instead of traveling the country in an RV.

A lesson from history

To drive this point home, consider this historical example. Imagine three individuals—Peter, James, and John— who each retired on January 1st in 3 consecutive years, starting in 1962, 1963, and 1964. Peter, James and John had all worked hard in the fishing industry, saved their money, and retired with $1,000,000 each. Each one of them allocated their funds into a 60-40 equity/bond portfolio and enjoyed a lovely 30-year retirement and withdrew $50,000 annually for retirement income. Given the similarities in their situations and the closeness in the timing of their retirements, you might think their account balances would be similar at the end of their retirements in 1991, 1992 and 1993, respectively.

However, this was not the case.

Year of Initial Withdrawal	Initial Portfolio Value	Initial Annual Income	Account Balance After 30 Years
1962	$1,000,000	$50,000	$122,800
1963	$1,000,000	$50,000	$1,704,000
1964	$1,000,000	$50,000	$896,700

Because the returns were negative in Peter's first year of retirement, the three men's ending account balances were significantly different. Peter never made up the losses of that first year and even more surprising, the returns of that one year put his entire retirement in jeopardy. Though all three men enjoyed the same 8% average return over the 30 years, James's and John's accounts faired considerably better because the returns at the beginning of their withdrawal period were positive rather than negative.

Your retirement success is critically dependent on the returns you earn at the beginning of your withdrawal period. In any effective retirement plan, contingencies need to be made and anticipated in order to protect your nest egg at this decisive stage.

CHAPTER 11

KEY #4: FEES REALLY DO MATTER

> *"Beware of little expenses; a small leak will sink a great ship."*
> — **Benjamin Franklin**

I remember when we bought our first home. My wife was pregnant with our first baby and we were going to bring her home to a sweet little crib in her own room and the perfect patch of grass in the backyard. We bought a one-story, three-bedroom house in a Phoenix suburb for $125,000.

Or at least that was the price the house was listed at. When we actually went in to sign the papers and buy the house, there were thousands of dollars of additional fees and taxes added on to the price of that cute little starter home. I was buying a house and everybody wanted their piece of that pie. There was a fee for the appraisal and the inspection and the credit report and the title service. There were government recording charges, origination fees, and rate fees. There were fees for the fees. Think up a fee and I'm sure it was tacked on there. But they were all listed in black and white and we signed our initials next to every one of them.

This is not how investment fees work. Recently, CNBC surveyed 10,000 households who used financial services and they reported that 51% didn't know what they paid in fees for those services. Now it may seem crazy that over half the people with financial investments don't know what they pay in fees, but I think that reported number is actually too low. I find that 9 out of 10 people who walk into my office are aware of some fees, but rarely do they know and understand all of the fees that are being charged against their accounts.

Finance is an area already charged with lots of ugly emotions like fear and shame and ignorance, and trying to figure out and understand the fees we are paying is just more evidence that we don't really know what we're doing. Fees are the fine print of an already confusing and overwhelming subject. So we put our heads in the sand, keep putting money away, and hope for the best. After all, everybody knows you can't get something for nothing; it takes money to make money, so whatever fees you're paying must need to be paid, right?

Most people have their expertise in something other than finances. They've spent their lives as a doctor or an engineer or a teacher. When the financial statement comes they glance over it, trying to discern just what it is they're seeing, but it's confusing and overwhelming. They file it away and hope they're not being taken to the cleaners. I'm here to tell you that what you don't know about fees can hurt you and your retirement plan. It's important to understand enough about fees to see if you are getting the bang for your buck. There are going to be fees in any investment. The key is to see if you're getting your money's worth.

401(K) fee structures

It turns out that 401(k)s are one of the biggest culprits when it comes to fees because many people view the 401(k) as a benefit provided by their company. 67% of Americans think they pay no fees at all on 401(k)s. But the truth is this "benefit" is not free—the average 401(k) fee is 3%—and most of the expenses are passed on to the employee. At the end of the day, the company only pays the administration costs associated with providing the plan to their employees.

The Center for American Progress estimates that an average American pays over $138,000 in fees over their lifetime. And the cost becomes much more exorbitant for those that earn more or save more inside their 401(k) plan. You took all of the risk, sacrificed the money to build up your 401(k) account, and then the fees take out a huge chunk. Ouch.

The devil is in the details

If there is one thing Wall Street is really good at it is hiding the true cost of a fund. But because they can't legally hide anything, they bury it in a mountain of other information so it is difficult to find or understand. We have all received the booklet of fine print for the various funds we are invested in and because we have "diversified" that adds up to a stack of the driest, most difficult reading you could ever imagine. As a result, most investors don't take the time to sort through all of the fine print to determine the total fees they are paying; and who could blame them? That's why you hired someone else to manage your account, right? This can be a critical mistake because those various fees really start to add up.

The Expense Ratio

The easiest fee to identify is the expense ratio. This ratio includes the management fee, which is the cost the fund manager charges to pick and adjust the holdings inside the fund. On average the management fee ranges between 0.5%-1% which means that the fund manager earns this whether the fund goes up or down. He doesn't even have to be good at his job.

In addition to management fees, the expense ratio includes "administrative costs" which include a whole host of things like postage and record keeping and coffee machines and 12B-1 fees, which is a marketing fee that goes toward paying broker commissions, as well as advertising and promoting the fund. You read that right. If you are paying the 12B-1 fee, you are paying the mutual fund to advertise itself.

All together the average expense ratios range from 0.2% (usually for index funds) to as high at 2%, but the average is somewhere around 1.4%.

Transaction Fees

It seems pretty straightforward to identify the expense ratio of various investment vehicles because these are the "visible" or reported costs. However, funds also have a mass of "invisible," unreported costs that are harder to detect and discover, the most notable one being transaction costs that occur when managers make changes in the portfolio makeup. The SEC does not require mutual funds to reveal these trading costs to investors.

In a study that analyzed portfolio holdings and transaction data for 1,800 equity funds from 1995-2006, researchers found that these "invisible costs" can actually be even higher than expense ratios and they have a considerable negative impact on fund performance. In the study, the funds' average transactions costs were 1.44% compared with their average expense ratio of 1.19%.[8] And the researchers concluded that there was "a strong negative relation between aggregate trading cost and fund return performance," specifically showing that funds with the highest transactions costs underperformed funds with the lowest transactions costs by 1.78% a year, nearly a 2% difference in returns.

Loads

Loads are fees that mutual funds use to compensate brokers for selling the fund. When you pay a load fee for a mutual fund, you are essentially paying the broker's commission.

Mutual funds are divided up into different classes, which is just the designation for how they charge the load fee. Class A mutual funds are front-end load funds, where a percentage is charged up front when you buy your shares. The average load for a Class A mutual fund is 5.75%. On the first day. Just for the privilege of joining their club, I guess. Class B mutual funds have back-end loads, where a percentage is charged when you sell the shares. Many times this percentage can vary depending on how long you leave your money in the fund, but it is usually between 1%-6%.

There are also mutual funds (Class C, institutional, and index) that generally do not charge a load. Keep in mind that even though you have been taught your whole life that A is better than C, there is no evidence that shows a correlation between paying a load and getting better fund performance.

To bring this home, I had a client who came into my office just last week. His 401(k) was spread over 5 different funds, with 20% of his money invested in each fund. One of these funds was an index fund with very low fees, another was a target-date fund, and the other three were large cap funds. As we charted the ups and downs of these five funds in the market, we found they had all followed the index fund almost exactly. He thought he was diversified by having his money in five different funds, but I was able to show him that they had all performed exactly the same as the benchmark. But even more importantly, I pointed out that while the other four funds were responding identically to the benchmark, they were actually costing him 7-8 times more money. When the fees were assessed, those four funds were actually underperforming the market, and he was paying good money to have them do so.

Double dipping

As if you weren't already being fleeced, there is also an opportunity for some brokers to "double dip." Many brokers and advisors charge a management fee to choose the investments and manage a portfolio. Double dipping occurs when the broker invests the portfolio into funds that also charge a load. If this happens, fees are stacked on top of fees resulting in a greater drag on the portfolio and hurting the performance of the investment.

Adding up the real cost

After factoring in expense ratios, transactions costs, and loads, many mutual funds have fees that total over 3%! But what if we can pick lower cost options and get our fees down to 1%. Will a reduction of 2% really make a difference in the overall performance of your portfolio? Let's take a look.

In the following example both investors contribute $300,000 and get average annual returns of 6%. Investor A moves his investments so that he only has fees of 1%, whereas Investor B leaves his money where it is and continues to pay fees of 3%. Over time, this one change will make a huge impact on Investor A's portfolio. Investor A will get to keep more than half a million dollars as a result of this "small" 2% change.

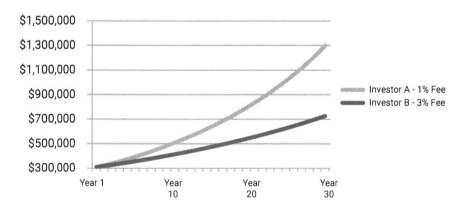

Perhaps you think you're too close to retirement for this change to make a difference. Keep in mind that retirement may last a long time. You may be in retirement for 20-30 years and your money will need to keep growing. If you look at this same comparison when you are making withdrawals on the account, the need for lower fees is even more apparent.

In this next chart everything remains the same except that now we start taking $12,000 a year out of the account. At the end of 30 years there is still a $342,000 difference in the accounts.

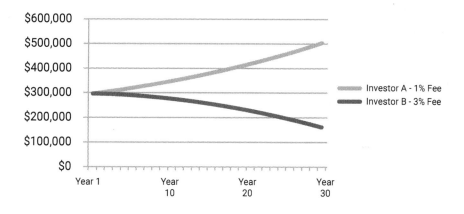

To drive this point home, the following chart reveals the impact just 1% can make on your retirement portfolio over your lifetime.

The Impact of Fees

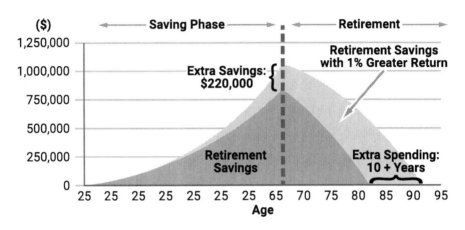

Source: AllianceBernstein[9]

Reducing fees by just 1% produces $220,000 in additional savings and an additional 10 years of income in retirement!

Fees and the value proposition

"But wait," you say, "I'm paying those fees for a reason. I pay fees so that I can have funds that perform well in the market. You get what you pay for, right?" Actually, in most cases, the exact opposite is true.

Every year Morningstar publishes an annual report and looks at how actively managed mutual funds are performing against the benchmark. They wrote, "Higher cost funds are more likely to underperform. **Fees matter. They are one of the only reliable predictors of success.**" In other words, the number one predictor for fund underperformance is the amount of fees being charged. The more the fund costs, the more likely they are to underperform. Keeping fees low is the number one thing you can do to make your portfolio successful.

At the end of the day, choosing to invest your money in a fund that has fees instead of a low cost index fund comes down to the value proposition we discussed in Chapter 5. You must ask the questions "Am I getting a better return, taking less risk, or both when compared to the index or benchmark? What did I pay to produce these results?

In some cases, it can be worth it to pay a little extra in fees if it improves performance or lowers risk. You need to evaluate what you are getting for that "little extra." For example, an index fund is going to follow the market, and though it is low-cost, its risk is substantial and the fund is susceptible to those 40% losses we saw in 2008. Investors that paid higher fees but were able to avoid these steep drops obviously came out ahead. If, however, your returns and your risks are comparable to cheaper vehicles, it makes more sense to pay less for the same outcomes.

Put your focus where it counts

Generally when people go to invest, they spend all their time trying to pick the very best funds and optimizing their asset allocations. Asset allocation is the "sexy" part of designing a portfolio and it's how managers justify their fees. The truth is that the fees involved are most likely offsetting any benefit of that work, no matter how good those investors are at their job.

Remember the number one indicator of portfolio performance is fee structure. Instead of putting your time into figuring out the perfect asset allocation plan, spend your time finding investments with smaller fees. It's not sexy. It may not be exciting. But it's where you will make the biggest impact on your portfolio.

I had a gentleman come into the office. He had invested $300,000 with an investment firm and the firm wasn't charging him a fee. He therefore thought he wasn't paying any fees at all. As we dissected his statement however, I showed him that he was invested in 23 different funds and each one of them was a Class A mutual fund with a 5.75% front-end load fee, meaning the day he bought the funds he paid $17,250 in up-front fees. In addition, each individual fund had a separate mutual fund management fee, an administrative cost, and a 12B-1 marketing fee, which added up to 1.3%, or $4,000 a year in fund management fees. The first year alone, he paid $21,000 in fees. With fees like that it's tough to keep yourself retired.

Therefore, what?

The reality is that there are always going to be fees. But you've got to do what you can to minimize those and get the most from your portfolio, always weighing those decisions according to the value proposition: what returns at what risk for what cost.

Always assume that your investments have fees and recognize that it's worth the effort to discover what those are. It's your money. Don't give it to someone else because you're too confused or too overwhelmed or too busy. Fees matter and have a huge impact on your returns and your account balances. This can't be overstated. They are the number one factor in your investment success.

CHAPTER 12

KEY #5: REDUCING TAXES TO MAKE YOUR MONEY LAST

"You must pay taxes. But there's no law that says you gotta leave a tip."
— **Morgan Stanley advertisement**

Taxes. We all hate them. But in a lot of cases I have found that people have a defeatist attitude when it comes to taxes. They just throw their hands in the air and say, "Well, I gotta pay them, right?"

While we all have to pay taxes, if we take the time to evaluate our financial situation, there are usually strategies and opportunities that we can implement to pay less. Now don't get me wrong. I am not recommending tax evasion as a retirement strategy. The IRS doesn't mess around and I'm pretty sure you don't want to spend your golden years in the Fed's country club. I'm talking about tax efficiencies—finding ways to recognize income at lower tax rates, timing the spending of tax-deferred assets, and creating tax "diversification."

If someone told you about a way to generate a 5-10% bonus return on your accounts, most of us would jump at the chance. Implementing an efficient tax strategy can produce those kinds of results. Whether it's a higher return or saving money on taxes, it's all the same. Both leave more money in your pocket and allow your retirement dollars to stretch further.

Tax-deferred accounts

If you have been saving for retirement, you have probably been saving a lot of that money in 401(k) or IRA accounts. And you are not alone. Today there is more than $25 trillion saved in tax-deferred accounts in the United States.

For years, we have been encouraged to save for retirement using tax-deferred accounts because most people have higher incomes while they are working than they do in retirement. Instead of paying taxes on your money when you earned it, these tax-deferred accounts allow you to pay the taxes only when the money is withdrawn and because your income is lower, hopefully you will pay at a much lower tax rate.

Additionally, there is an incentive to save in a 401(k) because many employers will match a certain percentage of the money you contribute to your 401(k) and wise savers will take advantage of this "free money."

The two determining factors for taxes

The amount you ultimately pay in taxes is determined by two factors: the amount of your income and the tax rate. According to the 2010 US Census, the average income for households ages 55-64 is $78,691. As individuals begin to retire, the average income drops to $50,121 for households over the age of 65. That is more than a $28,000 decrease in income, which should logically correlate with paying less in taxes, right? Not so fast.

While you may have much lower income in retirement, there is mounting evidence that your tax rate—that second factor—may be higher than it is today. Much higher. If we keep saving money in these tax-deferred accounts and tax rates then increase, we could be unintentionally creating a tax bomb waiting to explode. Let's take a look at a few fun facts to help reveal what the future tax picture might look like.

The United States is maxing out its credit cards

Our current national debt is nearly $20 trillion and half of that has accumulated over just the last 10 years. By 2020, the national debt is expected to rise to $22.5 trillion which is at a much faster pace than our gross domestic product (GDP). This is important because the debt-to-GDP ratio shows how leveraged a country is. A low debt-to-GDP ratio indicates an economy that can produce enough goods and services to pay back debts without borrowing more money. A high debt-to-GDP ratio indicates an economy that will be forced to borrow to pay back what it has already borrowed. In case you are wondering, this is not a good thing.

To put this in more relatable terms, a high debt-to-GDP ratio is like having a bunch of credit card debt that is coming due, but instead of saving up the money and paying them off, you do a balance transfer and move the debt to a new credit card. You may or may not get better terms on this transfer but it buys you some time. But we all know at some point the music will stop and the money must be paid back.

Near the end of World War II, due to heavy borrowing to build battleships, tanks, and arm soldiers, our country's debt-to-GDP ratio surpassed 100% for the first and only time.

Unfortunately, we are approaching those levels again and are expected to reach a debt-to-GDP of 100% by 2024.

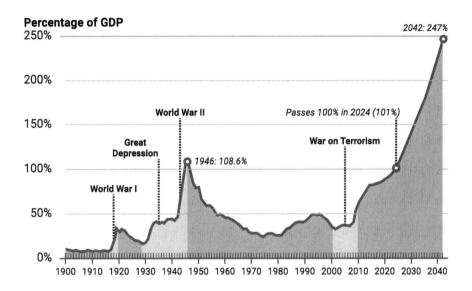

This debt ain't free

And of course, all that debt comes at a cost, namely interest. In the next 6 years, the cost of just the interest on our debt will more than double, and if it continues to rise as projected, we will be spending more on interest payments than we do for the entire Department of Defense. By 2020, the interest the US pays will account for 30% of total income tax revenue.

Cost of Interest on U.S. Debt

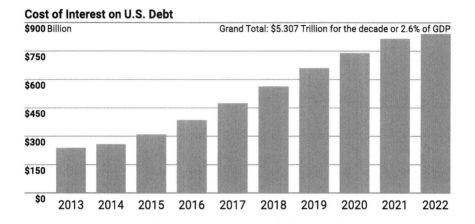

Not only that, but as we have already talked about, there is an increasing strain to fund entitlement programs. Unless changes or cuts are made to the Social Security program, by 2032 100% of all tax revenue will be needed just to cover the interest on the debt and pay for entitlement programs. No big deal. I'm sure we can get by without a military, a court system, or any federal employees.

All Tax Revenue Will Go Toward Health Care, Social Security, and Net Interest by 2032

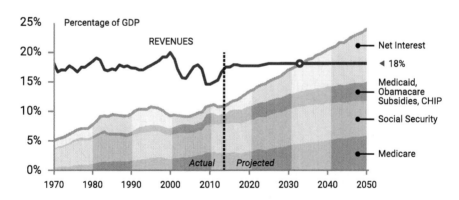

My crystal ball and the writing on the wall

After showing this heart-sinking information to my clients, I will often ask, "Would you be willing to bet me that taxes are going to go *down* in the future? What if I gave you 3:1 odds?" I have yet to have someone take that bet.

In this case, we can all look into our crystal ball and see with almost certainty that taxes must increase. The problem has become so large, so out of control, we are really left with no other options.

Now if you were in charge of the US government and you were trying to figure out how to pay for these major costs, what would you do? Remember, that there is over $25 trillion sitting in tax-deferred accounts. $25 trillion that hasn't been taxed yet. $25 trillion that could go a long way to paying down our debts. Is it too much of a leap to think that these deferred accounts may prove to be a little too tempting for Uncle Sam to ignore?

According to my crystal ball, our government really doesn't have much choice. Taxes are likely to increase dramatically which means that even though you may be making less money in retirement, your tax rate could actually be higher than it is while you are working. This means that all of your tax-deferred money will also be taxed at a higher rate. But how much higher? For that answer we must go back in time a little bit.

Back to the future

The last time our country saw an income tax cut was back in 2002. The Bush tax cuts were one of the largest tax cuts in our country's history. Under these cuts, tax rates were lowered across the board with tax rates starting at 10% (the first time a starting tax bracket was that low since 1941). Originally these tax cuts were set to expire in 2010 but were extended until 2012 and then made a permanent part of the "solution" Congress put into place as we stared down the fiscal cliff at the end of 2012. Beginning in 2013, only those in the highest income bracket received a tax increase.

As we discussed earlier, with the increasing deficit our country is facing, an increase in tax rates for more than just the top tier is not only possible, it is likely unavoidable. While it may be difficult to predict the exact changes to our current tax rates, it would not be unrealistic to assume that our tax rates could look similar to the levels we had before the Bush tax cuts went into effect in 2002.

So what did the tax rates in 2001 look like and how did they compare to our tax rates today?

2001 Tax Rates (Inflation Adjusted)

	Single		Married Filling Jointly	
Tax Rate	Over	But Not Over	Over	But Not Over
15%	$0	$35,068	$0	$58,598
27.5%	$35,068	$84,980	$58,598	$141,633
30.5%	$84,980	$177,284	$141,633	$215,852
35.5%	$177,284	$385,487	$215,852	$385,487
39.1%	$385,487	–	$385,487	–

2017 Tax Rates

	Single		Married Filling Jointly	
Tax Rate	Over	But Not Over	Over	But Not Over
10%	$0	$9,325	$0	$18,650
15%	$9,326	$37,950	$18,651	$75,900
25%	$37,951	$91,900	$75,901	$153,100
28%	$91,901	$191,650	$153,101	$233,350
33%	$191,651	$416,700	$233,351	$416,700
35%	$416,701	$418,400	$416,701	$470,700
39.6%	$418,401	–	$470,701	–

According to 2017 tax rates, income could be as high as $153,100 for a married couple and $91,900 for a single person and still be in a 25% tax bracket or lower. If taxes go back to what they were before the Bush tax cuts, income over just $58,598 for a married couple and $37,950 for singles, would put you in the 27.5% tax bracket! In this highly plausible scenario, many people could find themselves making less money but paying higher taxes; higher taxes on *all* income including the money they have been deferring taxes on all these years. Now that should make you justifiably sick to your stomach.

Steps to maximize your tax efficiency

So what steps can you take now to avoid this potential issue? There are a several options to consider that will allow you to proactively address this issue and optimize your financial plan.

WHILE WORKING: Tax-Deferred Contributions

As you contribute funds into your 401(k) or IRA plan, you are deferring the taxes on those funds to some point in the future. Depending on your current tax bracket, it may be better to pay some of those taxes now on some contributions rather than deferring all the taxes to a time when tax rates may be higher.

With that being said, if your employer matches a percentage of your contributions, make sure you contribute enough to take full advantage of the "free money" they will contribute into your account. For example, if your company matches 3% and you are contributing 12% but are concerned about future tax rate increases, then redirect the unmatched portion (9%) into another tax-free or after-tax savings bucket.

WHILE WORKING: Roth Accounts

More and more employers are providing tax-free options inside of their retirement plans as long as you don't make too much money and exceed the limits allowed by law. While you don't get a tax write-off today, the accumulated contributions and growth will be tax-free when withdrawn during retirement. Having a tax-deferred account, a tax-free account (such as a Roth IRA), and a regular taxable investment account will give you flexibility as to where to pull money from to supplement your income during retirement. Depending on your income level and the tax rates at the time, you can then determine which account to withdraw the money from to maximize tax efficiency.

Roth 401(k) plans, offered by many employers, have no income restrictions. If you are over 50, you can put $24,000 a year into one of these tax-free accounts. Again, you will not receive a tax break on the money contributed, but all the growth is tax-free.

WHILE WORKING & IN RETIREMENT: Conversion of Existing Retirement Accounts

Recently, most of the restrictions for converting funds from a tax-deferred account to tax-free accounts have been removed. This means that you can convert your existing IRA and 401(k) accounts into tax-free vehicles where all future growth and withdrawals will have no tax consequences. These conversions should be done when taxes are low and at amounts that don't push you into a higher tax bracket.

For example, let's assume you're an average retiree with taxable income of $50,000. This means that based on today's tax rate, you could convert about $25,000 from your tax-deferred accounts into tax-free vehicles and still remain in the 15% tax bracket. The taxes due from doing the conversion can be withheld from the money you converted or you can pay for the taxes from another account. If you pay the taxes from another account, all $25,000 will remain in the tax-free account which in turn will result in more tax-free growth.

Because most people will only be able to convert a small portion of their total tax-deferred savings each year and still remain in the same tax bracket, it is critical to begin executing this strategy as soon as possible. Each year that goes by is a lost opportunity to get more of your money into a tax-free account. By taking advantage of this opportunity, you are choosing to pay taxes today at likely a much lower rate rather than waiting and paying at a possibly higher tax rate in the future.

IN RETIREMENT: Income Strategies

During retirement you need to manage your income streams so that you withdraw the right amount of income to stay in desirable tax brackets. If possible, continue to defer pensions or Social Security benefits during the first few years of retirement and fund your income needs from your IRA accounts. This gives you lots of financial advantages.

Not only does this allow your Social Security and pension benefits to grow, it drops your income to zero or to a very low level, and puts you in a lower tax bracket. This, in turn, allows you to pull money from your IRA accounts at a lower tax rate and diffuse the tax bomb.

RMDs and you

Uncle Sam is happy to have you grow your retirement savings tax-deferred, but eventually he wants his money. It can't just grow there indefinitely. Starting at age 70½, the IRS requires you to take required minimum distributions (RMDs) from your tax-deferred accounts. This is the minimum amount of money that must be withdrawn from your account and taxed in a given year. The RMD is calculated by using the account balance divided by a "distribution period" that takes life expectancy into account. The RMD begins at about 3.5% and continues to go up every year.

2016 was the first year the oldest baby boomers started to take their RMDs and thankfully our tax rates are the lowest they've been in 35 years. As I've illustrated, this may not be the case for long. It's important to plan for times when the tax rates may be higher and affect the amount of the RMD that actually makes it into your pocket.

Money that grows in tax-free Roth IRA accounts is not subject to RMDs. This is another reason why having your money in several different buckets—tax-free, tax-deferred, and taxable—can reduce the amount of taxes you have to pay. This strategy reduces the overall amount that must be withdrawn through RMDs, effectively lowering your taxable income.

A case in point

I had a client who first came to see me when he turned 66. Because of a health issue, he was thinking of retiring. He could no longer do his job as a physician like he wanted to and was receiving long-term disability because of his health condition.

The long-term disability income he was receiving was tax-free and covered his income needs. He was getting ready to draw his Social Security benefits and retire. I explained that if he waited to retire until he was 70, it would increase his Social Security benefit by 8% each year (a great return by any standard) and also increase his wife's benefit. Then I mentioned that it would also allow him to be more tax efficient.

"What do you mean?" he asked.

I explained that by not drawing his Social Security and having his income needs met by his tax-free disability insurance, he effectively didn't have any taxable income. This obviously put him in a low tax bracket. He could then draw up to $75,000 a year out of his IRAs and put them into Roth IRAs, paying those taxes in the 15% tax bracket, whereas it was very likely that in the future he could be paying those taxes in the 27.5% bracket.

It's important when considering your tax strategy to look long range. Many times your accountant just wants you to pay the least amount of taxes today. I get that. Turns out I don't like paying taxes either. But sometimes it makes sense to pay a tax today in order to possibly reduce a larger tax bill down the road. In this case, this client saved over 12% on his tax bill, and that's as good as getting a 12% return on your money. Even if you can just reduce your taxes by paying them strategically by 5-10%, that's a 5-10% return on your money and any one of us would take that any day of the week.

Efficiency is key

For those that have a majority of their retirement nest egg in taxable IRA, 401(k), and other tax-deferred accounts, understanding how our current and future tax environments will affect you is critical to keeping more of your hard-earned money. While it may be difficult to pay a little more in taxes today, it is much better than the alternative. When taxes increase in the future, those that take advantage of this opportunity will have a variety of accounts, both taxable and tax-free, that can be used to maximize tax efficiencies. Having these options available will give you the ability to appropriately adjust and adapt your financial plan during retirement.

CHAPTER 13

KEY #6: EFFICIENT INCOME STREAMS

"Money is only a tool. It will take you wherever you wish, but it will not replace you as the driver."

— Ayn Rand

M y kids love to play board games. We are always looking for a new game to play but we often go back to the "oldies but goodies." One of the all-time classic games we go back to is *Jenga. Jenga* is a stacking game that consists of 54 wooden blocks. To start the game, the blocks are arranged in a tower with three blocks on each level. To play, each player takes a turn removing a block from the tower and stacking it carefully back on top of the tower without knocking the whole thing down. The person that makes a move that knocks the tower down loses.

In the beginning it's easy. You can move almost any block without too much thought or planning and the tower of blocks remains standing. But as the game progresses and the tower becomes more unstable, the moves become harder and harder. The moves you made earlier in the game often limit the moves available later on, and those early choices can make it difficult or impossible to make a move late in the game without the whole tower collapsing.

Managing your income streams in retirement is much the same. At the beginning pulling money from your nest egg is easy. It seems like it doesn't really matter where it is taken from or how much you withdraw. But—and this is critically important to understand—the moves you make at the beginning of retirement can impact your options later on. Pull money from the wrong account, spend too much, take Social Security benefits too early, or suffer a large loss at the beginning of your retirement and the effects could be devastating to your income years later. When it comes to retirement, pulling the right block at the right time can make all the difference.

The 4% rule

The amount of income you can generate in retirement depends on three factors: the amount you have, how fast you grow it, and how fast you spend it. Think about it like a garden full of seedlings. Your ability to feed yourself will depend on the amount of seedlings you start with, how fast they grow into fruit, and how fast you eat the harvest. If you get too hungry to wait for fruit, you end up eating your seedlings and soon the ground is bare.

To avoid outliving your money, a withdrawal rate from retirement accounts of 4% percent per year was traditionally recommended. This was considered a "safe rate" to withdraw money and provide income for life, without the risk of running out early. However, this rule is now being called into question.

Morningstar recently published a paper in which they stated that 4% was too high of a withdrawal rate if you expected funds to last 30 years. The reason for the change was the increased volatility as well as the historically low interest rates we have experienced over the past decade. In other words, the assumptions were wrong. Past performance is apparently not a predictor of future performance—isn't that the standard caveat? Additional research has revealed that using the 4% rule could lead to failure rates over 50%, meaning that more than half of all retirement accounts will run out of money by withdrawing 4% a year.[10]

Live long and prosper

Improved life expectancy has also caused the 4% rule to be called into question. Over the past 100 years we have seen the most dramatic increase in life expectancy with an increase of over 30 years. But those life expectancy figures only tell half the story.

Life expectancy is an average. If you have 100 people, some will die in childhood, some will die in mid-life, some will live over 100 years. All of these numbers are averaged together to give an "average" lifespan. But as these 100 people get older, those who died young and lowered the life expectancy average have already passed away, meaning that there is a high probability that those who are still alive at 65 will live much longer than the average life expectancy. I mean, someone's bringing up the average, right?

The chart below demonstrates this. If you are already 65, there is a 47% probability that either you or your spouse will live into your 90s. This means that a 30-year retirement is not only a distinct possibility, it is a quantifiable probability.

If you're 65 today, the probability of living to a specific age or beyond

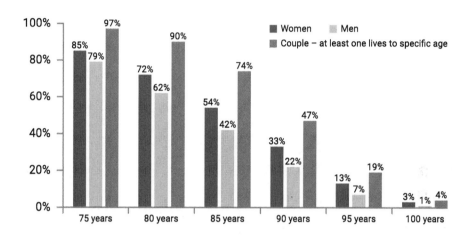

Sequence of returns review

As we discussed in Chapter 10, the sequence of returns matters. As a reminder, when you begin taking withdrawals from your retirement accounts, the sequence (or order) of positive and negative annual returns is often the most important factor in determining how long your money will last. As I demonstrated, large losses at the beginning of retirement will significantly increase your chance of running out of money. Because of the low interest rates over the past 10 years, retirees have been taking more risk in order to generate a higher return, which in turn, has exposed more accounts to the impact of the sequence of returns.

The best way to mitigate the risks of sequence of returns is to not make withdrawals from accounts with negative returns. In other words, if at all possible, avoid pulling that block from your retirement income tower. As you near retirement, set aside enough income in no-risk accounts to outlast a possible period of negative returns. Another option is to avoid negative returns altogether.

Income efficiency

So, if you want to avoid negative returns or your retirement income tower is teetering and you're worried about running out of money, what should you do? The answer for many is to use an annuity. As we talked about in Chapter 7, annuities have pros and cons but one of their best features is that they are extremely efficient in generating income. **In other words, they can produce more income with less money.** Annuities allow you to withdraw money at a higher withdrawal rate (often greater than 4%) while also guaranteeing that you will never run out of money. They do this by spreading out risk.

To understand this, let's take homeowner's insurance as an example. Let's say you own a $300,000 home that you want to insure. You call around and get several quotes ranging from $500 to $700 per year so you pick the best policy and put it in place. But have you ever wondered how an insurance company can insure your home worth $300,000 and only charge you $700 per year? If your house burned down and they had to rebuild it from the ground up, it seems like $700 a year isn't nearly enough to cover that large of an expense.

The reason they can do it is because of something called risk diversification. The insurance company has access to mountains and mountains of data that allows them to predict with almost certainty the chance a claim will be filed, the cost of the average claim, and the chance of a total loss claim. Using this data, they can predict with pinpoint accuracy how many policies they need to issue and how much to charge to cover the expected claims. They know that most policies will never have a claimed filed and those premiums can cover the claims made on a few of the issued policies. As a result, thousands of homes can be covered by the same insurance company and everyone is able to pay a reasonable amount to protect against the risk of loss.

This same concept works for generating income. The reason we can't just spend whatever we want from our retirement accounts is because we don't know how long our accounts need to last. We have no idea if our nest egg needs to cover 10 years or 30 years. But just like homeowners insurance, insurance companies can calculate with pinpoint accuracy the life expectancy probability of a group of people. As a result, they can guarantee a lifetime income for the entire group while also allowing them to spend or withdraw more from their accounts. In other words, they can diversify the risk allowing you to generate more income with less money.

To illustrate, let's take $100,000 and see how much income can be generated depending on how it is invested. The first $100,000 is invested in a typical investment account made up of stocks and bonds. Because it is exposed to sequence of returns and longevity risk we will follow the advice of Morningstar and withdraw only 3.5% each year. The other investment is invested in an annuity. Because the insurance company is diversifying the risks listed above we will be able to withdraw 5% each year.

	Stock/Bonds	Annuity
Investment:	$100,000	$100,000
Withdrawal Rate:	3.5%	5.0%
Annual Income:	$3,500	$5,000

Due to the income efficiencies of an annuity, the same investment is able to generate 43% more income. And maybe more importantly, the account is guaranteed to generate income for life, completely eliminating longevity risk.

Income efficiency isn't free

As we discussed in Chapter 7, it is important to take a moment to review the limitations and restrictions of an annuity before you start thinking that they will solve all of your needs in retirement. Remember, the insurance company is only able to diversify longevity risk because they control how and when money can be taken from the accounts. Surrender schedules and charges allow them to restrict how and when funds are withdrawn and must be taken into account when designing a retirement plan.

In addition, depending on how you choose to take income from the annuity will determine whether you can access the lump sum in the future. All annuities allow you to annuitize. If you choose to annuitize, the insurance company will usually allow you to take money out at an even higher withdrawal rate (usually 6-8%) but the money is no longer available as a lump sum but instead will be paid out over the life of the annuitant. Because most people don't want to forfeit their money should they pass away early, more and more people are electing to add an income rider that will allow them to generate lifetime income and still pass on any remaining balance to their beneficiaries.

The rise of the income rider

If I asked the people I meet with day in and day out what features they would like to see in the perfect investment, at the top of most lists would be an investment that can't take a loss, never runs out of money, and passes any money left over to the beneficiaries. This is exactly what an income rider* is designed to do—which is why they have become increasingly popular.

While there are many different income riders and they all have different bells and whistles, this optional rider usually guarantees two things: a rate of return and a lifetime income. The guaranteed rate of return is generally calculated in two different ways. The first method, called a "set interest rate," simply increases the income value of the annuity by a set percentage every year no matter how the annuity itself actually performs. If the set interest rate is 7% but the annuity only earned 5%, the income value of the annuity would go up by 7%. This would happen every year regardless of performance.

The interest can also be added to the income value using a "stacking" rate of return. With a stacking income rider, interest is guaranteed to grow by the actual annuity

* Riders are available for an additional fee - some riders may not be available in all states.

performance *plus* an additional set interest rate *added on top* of the performance. For example if the annuity earned 5% as before, but had a stacking income rider of 4%, the income value would increase by 9%. Or if the performance was 2%, the income value would rise by 6%.

Account value vs. income value

So, you're probably asking how in the world an insurance company can guarantee that kind of growth and still stay in business. What's the catch? It is important to understand that when you add an income rider to an annuity, the insurance company calculates two values: the *account value* and the *income value*.

The account value grows based on the actual investment performance. A fixed annuity grows based on a fixed rate, an index annuity grows based on the chosen index, and the variable annuity grows based on the securities chosen. (See Chapter 7 for more details on the investment choices, risks, and fees for each different annuity.) The growth is added to the original investment minus any withdrawals to determine the account value. This value is available as a lump sum after the surrender period, or at death, whichever comes earlier.

When you add an income rider to the annuity, the income value is now calculated using a *set* or *stacking* rate. Because this growth is generally higher than the account value growth, the income value is almost always higher than the account value. The main difference is that the income value is never available as a lump sum—not at the end of the surrender period or even at death. Instead, this higher value can only be accessed by lifetime income payments. Remember, the insurance company can guarantee the higher growth rate, higher withdrawal rate, and do it for life because they know with remarkable accuracy how long a group of people will live. While the income value is not available for lump sum payout, any remaining balance in the account value at the time of death is passed on to the designated beneficiaries.

The price of peace

As you can see, income riders have several benefits: guaranteed returns, higher withdrawal rates, and lifetime incomes that can't be outlived. That doesn't mean they come without a cost. Income riders usually cost between .5% and 1.25% per year and you can only access up to 10% of your principal per year without penalty. The key is determining where these features can be used and properly allocating assets according to your income needs.

Critics of annuities argue that the real price you pay is smaller returns. They scoff at trading your peace of mind for "meager" or limited returns and recommend taking your chances in the market. Again, what they are missing is the power of income efficiency.

For example, let's take a $100,000 investment that we invest for 10 years before triggering an annual income. For Investment #1 we will invest the $100,000 in the market and let's assume you are able to generate an 8% average return. For Investment #2 we will choose an annuity that generates a return of 5% with no rider. Investment #3 will be invested in an annuity with a 7% income rider.

	Investment #1	Investment #2	Investment #3
Investment:	$100,000	$100,000	$100,000
Rate of Return:	8.0%	5.0%	7.0%
Balance After 10 Years:	$215,892	$162,889	$196,715

Now, it's time to withdraw income. Using Morningstar's recommended 3.5% withdrawal rate for Investment #1 and a 5% withdrawal rate for the two annuity investments, how much income does each investment generate?

	Investment #1	Investment #2	Investment #3
Account Balance:	$215,892	$162,889	$196,715
Withdrawal Rate:	3.5%	5.0%	5.0%
Annual Income (Year 11):	$7,556	$8,144	$9,836

In this example, even though the annuity investments had a lower rate of return, both produce more income than the stock investment. In fact, for the stock investment to match the income produced by the annuity with the income rider, it would require an annual rate of return of 10.89%! Additionally, no matter how long you live, the income from Investment #3 is guaranteed even if the account balance becomes exhausted. Clearly, you won't get that same offer from the stock market.

The untold hobbit tale

Let me use an example to explain how this works. Let's say Bilbo is going on a grand retirement adventure. In order to prepare for this adventure he buys a $100,000 annuity that grows at an average of 4% per year over a 10-year-period. If Bilbo takes no withdrawals, he will have an account value of $148,024 to take on his journey to defeat the dreaded dragon Smaug.

But, if Bilbo adds an income rider to his annuity, and is guaranteed to receive 6% a year over the same 10-year-period, his income value would be $196,715—$48,691 more than the account value (or surrender value). Bilbo now has a choice. He can take the $148,024 and head straight for the Lonely Mountain, or alternatively, he can receive the larger income value as a lifetime income stream. These annual income payments will continue to be paid no matter how long Bilbo lives, even if he learns the secrets of the elves and lives so long he exhausts the base annuity value. With an income rider, Bilbo can never outlive his money.

Let's say Bilbo chose a stacking rider rather than a set interest rate. If the very same market had averaged the same 4%, but Bilbo had a stacking income rider of 4% on his annuity, he would have earned 8% over the 10 years, and would have $215,892 that he could choose to receive in annual income payments. That amounts to $67,868 more than the lump sum payout option. Additionally, not only is Bilbo able to earn this money at a guaranteed rate, he can withdraw income to fund his adventure at a higher rate—as much as 50-100% higher—than if he had put his $100,000 in a Middle-earth mutual fund.

Wait a minute, though. What if Bilbo meets with a tragic end in an orc battle just as he starts to receive those annual payments? If Bilbo dies before the account value in the annuity is completely used, the remaining account balance will be passed on to his beneficiary, Frodo, at the time of his death. (In this case, I think it comes with a ring as well, but that's a story for another day.)

Additionally, even though Bilbo was not married, let's assume for a moment that he was. Bilbo could have selected a joint life payout so if he meets an untimely death, Mrs. Bilbo could still count on that income for the remainder of her life!

It comes down to the choice between a maybe and a guarantee. Income riders guarantee that your income value will grow by a fixed rate (usually between 5-8%) regardless of market conditions, and then at some point in the future that income value can be triggered as a lifetime income stream. For retirees facing a future dependent on an uncertain market, this can be an incredible relief.

Choose wisely

There is a scene in *Indiana Jones and the Last Crusade* when Indiana Jones has finally found the room where the Holy Grail is kept. On the stone shelves around the room are dozens of chalices, many imposters, and one true grail hidden among them. The knight who protects the Grail explains to Dr. Jones that he must choose the right cup, "But choose wisely, for while the true Grail will bring you life, the false Grail will take it from you."

Then the villain of the movie enters the room. He scans the various different grails and chooses one of pure gold, covered in jewels, the grail he thinks is "fit for a king." He drinks from the golden chalice, but the knight says, "You have chosen poorly," and the villain withers and dies. Indiana looks at all the cups and selects an old wooden chalice, dips it into the water and drinks. The knight replies, "You have chosen wisely."

When it comes down to it, retirement is simply figuring out how to replace your paycheck without working. Don't be distracted by the claims of high returns—the flashy, gold cup—but instead keep in mind the power of income efficiency. You have lots of choices to make in order to replace that income and if you do it right, you will be able to live on those income streams forever. (Even if you happen to stumble across an ancient wooden chalice that holds the power of eternal life.)

CHAPTER 14

STRATEGIES FOR HIGH NET WORTH INDIVIDUALS

*"It's not how much money you make,
but how much money you keep,
how hard it works for you, and how
many generations you keep it for."*
— Robert Kiyosaki

My sister has four children, and one of them recently graduated and left home. She shared a conversation with me that she had with another mother when she was bemoaning the fact that her son was growing up and leaving. The other woman brushed off her concerns saying, "Oh, it doesn't matter for you. After all, you have three more kids at home." My sister, who was in the deep throes of grief at the idea of *any* of her children leaving the nest, was completely taken aback. Sure, she had three other wonderful children at home, but that didn't change the fact that her oldest was indeed leaving, that she had birthed and cared for him for eighteen years, and he would never really be her little boy again. "If anything," she said, "it just made me think, 'Hey, wait a minute, they're *all* going to leave. I have to lose four of them. My loss isn't less...it's more.'"

Now admittedly, my sister can be a little melodramatic, and many of us are looking forward to the day our children finally head out on their own. But, in many ways, the retirement concerns of people with high net worth are treated just as indifferently. There is little sympathy for those who have amassed a lot of wealth, and no longer face the fear of running out of money, but instead worry about losing half of it to taxes. Somehow there's a feeling out there that if you have a lot of money you won't mind losing it as much as someone who has less. After all, you've got plenty more where that came from.

The reality is that even if you have a lot of money, it's still all rightfully yours. And you ought to put strategies in place to be able to keep as much as possible.

It's not what you make, it's what you keep

When meeting with high net worth clients, I am always amazed at how many of them have financial plans that have failed to protect their assets from the biggest danger they will face—*taxes*. Unfortunately, more often than not, little to nothing has been done to properly allocate assets into investments designed to keep more of their hard-earned money in their pocket instead of Uncle Sam's. Just as I mentioned in Chapter 12, there is a tendency to just shrug and give up, assuming that nothing can be done about it. As a result, thousands if not hundreds of thousands of dollars are being lost due to tax inefficiencies.

A review of the federal tax rates that wealthy investors pay will quickly reveal some key takeaways that can significantly improve the post-tax return you are seeking.

Federal Tax Rates for Wealthy Investors (Income: Individual - $200,000+, Married - $250,000+)			
Tax Category	Highest Federal rate	Affordable Care Surcharge	Total
Ordinary Income	39.6%	3.8%	43.4%
Short-term Capital Gains	39.6%	3.8%	43.4%
Long-term Capital Gains	20.0%	3.8%	23.8%
Qualified Dividends	20.0%	3.8%	23.8%
Non-Qualified Dividends	39.6%	3.8%	43.4%

As you can see from the chart, there are two tax categories that have a significantly lower tax rate than the other forms of income. Long-term capital gains and qualified dividends are taxed at a 23.8% rate while all other income is taxed at a 43.4% rate, an astounding 82% higher! Keep in mind that these tax rates do not include the additional state capital gains tax, which averages about 5.31%. Added together, all of these taxes take a significant toll on your returns.

The key takeaways from this are:

A properly designed portfolio will be structured to maximize growth in the tax categories with the lowest tax rates.

Strategies that avoid the realization of gains altogether should be utilized as much as possible.

While these takeaways should seem very straightforward and obvious, the portfolios of high net worth clients reveal very few differences when compared to others in far lower tax brackets. Nothing has been done to minimize the loss of their money to taxes—money that should still be in their pockets but which has been lost due to improper portfolio design.

For example, let's assume you earn a pre-tax return of 15% on a short-term capital investment. If we assume that the return is subject to the highest federal tax rate plus the average state tax rate, the total tax on that return would be 48.71%.

After factoring in the taxes due on this investment, your fabulous pre-tax return of 15% actually generates a post-tax return of 7.7%.

Now let's see what things would look like if this investment was held for at least a year and was taxed at the lower federal long-term tax rate of 23.8% with a total tax of 29.1%. Using the lower tax rate your pre-tax return of 15% generates a post-tax return of 10.6%, resulting in almost 38% more money in your pocket. In fact, it would require a pre-tax return of only 10.85%, or 4.15% less, to generate the same 7.7% post-tax return of the short-term capital gain investment.

For high net worth investors, post-tax returns and not pre-tax returns must be the focus. Remember, it's not what you make, it's what you keep.

The rules keep changing

I believe that tax efficiency is often ignored for one main reason: the tax code is always changing. This is challenging because you are trying to design a long-term investment approach using a moving target. Depending on who wins the election or what tax rates Congress finally agrees upon, impacts the design of the portfolio. For example, capital gains rates dropped from 35% in 1979 to 28% and finally to 20% in 1982. That was a decrease of over 40% in just four years! A welcome change for sure, but one that would have caused a dramatic shift in portfolio design in order to take advantage of the new tax rates.

Historical Highest Tax Rates

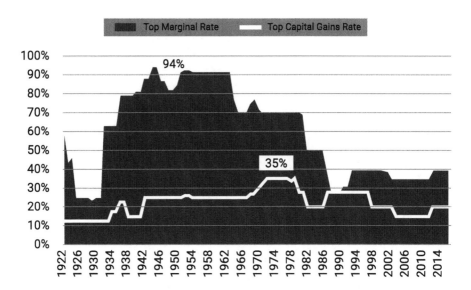

As the graph above illustrates, fluctuations in the highest marginal tax rate and capital gains tax rate have varied dramatically. This can be a significant problem because as I illustrated earlier, investing for the long-term is generally going to create better tax efficiencies. If you are constantly shifting the portfolio design every time the various tax rates drop or increase, the costs associated with realizing gains as part of the reallocation could be very costly. So, what is one to do? It seems you are caught between the proverbial "rock and a hard place."

While we cannot predict the exact ups and downs of the tax code, a few things can be reasonably assumed regarding capital gains taxation. First, long-term capital gains will be treated more favorably and will likely be taxed at a lower rate than short-term. Second, long-term capital gains will most likely be lower than ordinary income tax rates. And finally, because of the increasing national debt and funding issues, it is likely that all taxes will rise from their current levels (see Chapter 12). If we use these assumptions as the overriding guidelines when designing a portfolio, we can avoid much of the reallocation that could potentially destroy the tax efficiencies we are seeking.

In it for the long haul

Hopefully by now, you can see why a long-term approach to investing is so important for high net worth clients. Contrary to other investors, active and tactical management strategies are often not beneficial to high net worth individuals. While they may have lower volatility and risk, they will likely not generate enough in returns to offset the inefficiencies they generate when it comes to taxes. Now, you may be thinking, "But wait a minute, what about 'stage of life investing' and 'don't lose it in the first place'? How can I do both?"

The advantage that high net worth clients have over other investors is that they have more resources available to them to generate the income they need. If one asset is down due to a downturn in the market, they can patiently wait for those investments to recover and instead spend from another account. Because it is highly likely that a significant amount of their assets will never be needed and are likely to pass on to their beneficiaries, they can afford to ignore much of the volatility of the market and only shift the portfolio in order to avoid the large market corrections.

So, how do you know when to shift or stay? Knowing when to adjust or when to stay is determined by weighing the tax consequences of shifting the portfolio and paying taxes on the gains that would be realized with the alternative of holding course and absorbing a loss.

Let's look at an example to illustrate this. Let's say you invest $100,000 in a tech stock that doubles in six months. You may be thinking, "Time to sell before this stock comes back down to earth." The problem is that if you sell the stock before holding it for a year, your capital gains tax rate would be 48.71% or a cost of $48,710. If you waited just six more months, you would have held the stock for a year and your tax rate would drop to 29.1% or a cost of $29,100. Effectively, this means that the stock could fall $19,610 before the loss would have had a greater negative effect on your account balance than the capital gains taxes. (In a minute, I will show you how you can actually drop the tax rate to 0% saving the entire $48,710.)

Now, I realize this is an extreme example but it illustrates the fact that tax consequences should be treated like a transaction cost. The rule of thumb is that adjusting the portfolio is justified if the loss is anticipated to be larger than the cost of generating a taxable gain. In other words, if making a move nets more money than staying put after *all* costs are factored in, especially the tax consequences, then you are justified in making the move.

Additional strategies

Paying lower taxes is always nice but is it possible to eliminate taxes all together? The answer to this is yes. There are several strategies that can be utilized to limit or avoid taxes altogether.

Tax-loss harvesting

A common strategy that can be used to offset taxes is tax-loss harvesting. Tax-loss harvesting occurs when a security that has experienced a loss is sold resulting in the loss being realized, or "harvested." This loss can then be used to offset the taxes on other gains or income. Tax-loss harvesting can significantly reduce your taxes but proper execution to maximize the benefits takes some understanding and planning.

The first step is to determine your capital gains and then identify those holdings that would be good candidates to offset those gains. Remember, priority should be given to short-term gains as they are taxed at higher marginal rates (as much as 20% more) so you will get more bang for your buck by applying capital losses to these gains. In addition to looking at the type of gain, you can also identify assets that no longer fit your strategy or that you were going to sell anyway. Implementing tax-loss harvesting in tandem with portfolio rebalancing is a natural fit.

Once you have harvested capital losses, the next step is to determine which gains to offset. Short- and long-term losses must first be used to offset gains of the same type. After matching your gains and losses up, if you have more losses of one type they can be applied to the other type of gain. For example, if you have excess long-term losses of $25,000, they can be applied to offset any short-term gains. Applying excess long-term losses to short-term gains is the best way to maximize tax savings. If you have excess losses after all gains have been offset, up to $3,000 can be used to offset ordinary income.

Tax-loss harvesting should not change your overall investment objective or portfolio allocation, which means that a security is either repurchased or replaced by a similar security to keep the optimal asset allocation. But it is important that doing so doesn't create a "wash sale." The IRS won't just let you sell and then buy back the same holding just to save taxes. (They seem to think of everything.) The IRS has established specific rules on the sale and repurchase of securities. The rule states that that you cannot take a loss on an investment and then buy the same or "substantially identical" security within 30 days—before or after—of selling the loss-generating investment.

Because the IRS is so easy to work with they haven't defined what "substantially identical" actually means. Of course you can wait out the 30 days and then repurchase the security, but you are running the risk of the asset you just sold appreciating while you are sitting on the sidelines. Another option is to use ETFs for tax-loss harvesting which allows you to replace an ETF that is highly correlated to the ETF you just sold but that tracks a different index. The IRS has begun to set the precedent that ETFs of different indexes are not substantially identical and can be used to immediately replace a security that is sold.

Stepped-up cost basis

One of the most beneficial tax strategies for high net worth individuals is taking advantage of the step-up in basis rule. Step-up in basis is the readjustment of an asset to current market value at the death of an individual. If an asset can be held until death instead of selling prior it will provide significant tax savings because the appreciated asset is reevaluated and adjusted up to the value of the asset at the time of death rather than the time of purchase. Unlike some tax strategies that either reduce or defer taxes, taking advantage of the stepped-up cost basis can allow securities and real estate to transfer to a beneficiary while avoiding 100% of the taxes. For assets that have appreciated over time, this can result in huge savings.

For example, if a home was purchased for $200,000, but it is worth $400,000 when the owner passes away, the value of the home would be stepped-up to $400,000. In other words, if the beneficiary immediately sold the home for $400,000, there would be no capital gains due on the home. The same tax laws apply to securities. If $100,000 was used to purchase stock at $10/share and the stock appreciates to $20/share, there would be a capital gain of $100,000 if the stock was sold. But if the stocks are held until death, and sold at current market value, $20/share, no taxes for capital gains would be due.

As we discussed before, tax-loss harvesting allows you to essentially defer capital gains tax to a future date but in most cases the taxes will come due if the overall asset base continues to appreciate. But if we use the stepped-up basis rule in tandem with tax-loss harvesting even the deferred taxes can be avoided. As long as the assets used as part of the tax-loss harvesting are sold or transferred after the death of the individual, all of the deferred capital gains tax will be eliminated and completely avoided.

Municipal bonds

Another option is to look for tax-free investment strategies so that the tax liability is never created in the first place. Unfortunately, most high net worth clients never meet the requirements to be able to contribute to a Roth IRA or the benefits of doing a Roth conversion never outweigh the taxes that would be due. The good news is that municipal bonds* are often a perfect option for capturing tax-free growth that does not have the limitations and rules that exclude high net worth individuals.

A municipal bond is a debt security issued by a state, municipality or county. Essentially, when you buy a municipal bond, you are loaning money to the government entity. Like most bonds, you will receive interest from these bonds and when the bond reaches maturity your original investment is returned to you. What makes municipal bonds special and highly advantageous to high net worth clients is that municipal bonds are exempt from federal taxes and most state and local taxes as well. This means the interest they generate will not be reduced to pay taxes. It is one of the few tax-free income streams available to high net worth clients that can generate steady income at a lower risk.

Now keep in mind that municipal bonds still have risk and are impacted by fluctuating interest rates so it is important to properly design the municipal bond portfolio. These bonds are guaranteed by the ability of the government entity to pay

---

* Municipal bonds generate tax-free income, and therefore pay lower interest rates than taxable bonds. Therefore, municipal bonds may not be suitable for all investors. Please see your tax professional prior to investing.

the interest and return the original investment and you don't have to look too hard to find examples of cities and states (remember Detroit) that have had financial problems that have impacted bondholders.

In addition, like other bonds, if the bond must be liquidated before the term ends, the value of the bond can change because of interest rate fluctuations. If interest rates rise, for example, municipal bond prices will decline. You also must be able to find a buyer and some municipal bonds can be fairly illiquid which essentially ties up your money until the end of the term. Properly designing the bond portfolio by diversifying the holdings and varying the term lengths can go a long way to reducing the impact of these risks on the portfolio.

Tax-deferred investments

The key benefit tax-deferred accounts have over other accounts is that all earnings grow free of current federal, state, and local income taxes until the time they are withdrawn. This benefit allows you to earn interest on funds that would have already been paid in taxes. The extra interest that is generated will result in a higher after-tax value depending on the ordinary income tax rate at the time the funds are withdrawn. As shown in the following graph, the tax-deferred account generates significantly higher returns than the account that pays taxes as the growth accrues.

Taxable vs. tax-deferred investing over a 30-year time frame

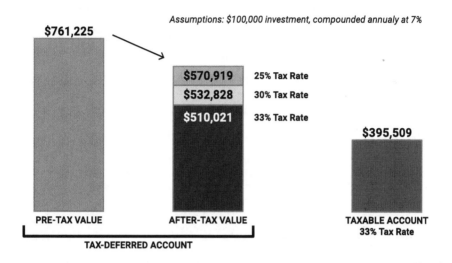

Assumptions: $100,000 investment, compounded annualy at 7%

$761,225		
	$570,919	25% Tax Rate
	$532,828	30% Tax Rate
	$510,021	33% Tax Rate
		$395,509
PRE-TAX VALUE	AFTER-TAX VALUE	TAXABLE ACCOUNT 33% Tax Rate
TAX-DEFERRED ACCOUNT		

Qualified accounts, which are tax-deferred, have rules regarding how much can be contributed each year, limiting the amount that can be sheltered in tax-deferred accounts. However, non-qualified annuities allow funds to grow tax-deferred and there is no limit on how much can be invested in these types of accounts. As discussed in Chapter 7, there are several different types of annuities to choose from depending on the overall objective and goal of the investment.

Tax strategies and life insurance

High net worth individuals are generally "self-insured," meaning they have enough assets to take care of those left behind should they pass away, but that does not mean they should not consider life insurance as part of a tax-efficient plan. Remember that tax-deferred accounts, such as IRAs or non-qualified annuities, will pass on to beneficiaries at ordinary income tax rates. When this happens, beneficiaries have two options: they can spread out payments and taxes or they can take the funds as a lump sum and pay all of the taxes at once. This is where life insurance can be used.

For example, I have a client who has more than $1M saved in IRA accounts. Over the past several years, she has taken her required minimum distributions (RMDs) but the accounts have continued to increase because they have been growing faster than the required withdrawals. Because all of this money has been tax-deferred, if she passed away there would be nearly $400,000 due in ordinary income tax. That's a pretty hefty bill she would be leaving to her kids and it would significantly reduce the amount each of them would actually receive.

Rather than do nothing and let Uncle Sam raid her kids' inheritance, we put a life insurance policy in place with an annual premium of $12,000 that she funded using part of her RMD. At her death, the policy will payout a $400,000 tax-free death benefit to her children which they can then use to pay all of the taxes that would be due and keep the entire $1M. Essentially she was pre-paying her tax bill using the life insurance. If she pays on the policy for 10 years, she would have only spent $120,000 to generate $400,000 in tax-free income. Even after 40 years, she would come out ahead because the money is tax free.

The same strategy can be used to mitigate estate taxes as well. The federal estate and gift tax exemption is $5.45M per individual, $10.9M for a married couple. Any estate over this exemption amount is subject to estate taxes, which have rates up to 40% plus additional state estate taxes where applicable. Joint life insurance policies are some of the cheapest life insurance you can buy because it is based on two lives instead of just one. The tax-free life insurance benefit is paid at the death of the last surviving spouse, and can be used to provide the money to pay the estate tax. Again, in almost every case the cost of a joint life policy over the life of the couple will be much lower than the cost of the estate taxes that will be due.

There are many other strategies that can be implemented while a client is alive to mitigate the effects of the estate tax. For example, the tax code allows for a tax-free annual gift exclusion of $14,000 per person. Other strategies include irrevocable trusts, CRUTs, CRATs, and Family Limited Partnerships. A knowledgeable advisor who pays attention to your portfolio's tax efficiency can help explore these options with you.

The hand in the cookie jar

For high net worth individuals, a financial plan's success hinges on tax efficiency. At the end of the day everything else is secondary because it's not what you make, it's what you keep that really matters. Tax efficiency is the key. It must be the priority and the driving factor in the design and management of the portfolio. Without a plan, the tax man cometh and he taketh as much as he wanteth.

When Philip Seymour Hoffman died suddenly in 2014, he was worth nearly $35 million dollars. Unfortunately there was not a tax-efficient plan in place and so the estate became subject to the maximum tax bill. His entire estate was left to his long-time partner, but because they were not married, only $5.45M of his estate was tax exempt. After that, a tax of up to 40% was levied on the excess. To make matters worse, he was a resident of New York which has its own estate tax, of up to 16% on the assets left to non-spouses and only provides a $1 million exemption. All totaled, Hoffman's estate owed a combined estate tax of more than $15.1 million. Worse still, because the marital deduction did not apply, any assets that remain when Hoffman's partner dies could get taxed again.

Don't fall into the trap of hopeless thinking when it comes to taxes. Don't believe the fiction that taxes must be paid and there is nothing you can do about it. Nothing could be further from the truth. As we have discussed, there are multiple options for lowering the amount of taxes that must be paid which in turn leaves more money in your pocket and in your estate. Whether it's your first dollar or your last, they're still *your* dollars. Put a plan in place to keep as many of them as possible for you and for those you will someday pass your estate to.

CHAPTER 15

NAVIGATING THE NEW RETIREMENT

"It's a round trip. Getting to the summit is optional, getting down is mandatory."

— **Ed Viesturs, the first American to climb Everest**

Preparing for retirement is often compared to climbing a mountain. For years, you struggle in an uphill battle, working and saving until you reach the pinnacle. When you finally reach the peak, you drop your pack, rest from your effort, and then coast all the way down. Right?

As I've shown in this book, the reality is that in the last decade or so we have entered a new kind of retirement. The landscape has changed. There is uncertainty and possible changes on the horizon for Social Security, pensions have disappeared for most Americans, replaced by the 401(k) and the IRA, which puts you firmly in charge of the accumulation and distribution of your retirement income.

Navigating this new landscape is not easy. In fact, rather than finally reaching the summit and coasting down, some of your most important work is just beginning. Just as a mountain is most dangerous at the steep pinnacle, those last few years before retirement and the critical first years entering it are often the most challenging, littered with the most pitfalls, and susceptible to mistakes that are hard to recover from.

As a kid, I remember reading a book from the school library about Mount Everest and the various attempts that had been made to reach its summit. Some attempts were successful while others ended in tragedy. Everest captured my imagination then and I have remained fascinated ever since. As I have worked with people helping them prepare and enter into retirement, I have found that the story of Everest holds several keys that can be applied to navigating a successful retirement.

The history of Everest

Attempts to summit Everest began in the 1920s. Fifteen different expeditions over the course of 30 years tried and failed to conquer the mountain. But, on May 29, 1953, two men, Edmund Hillary and Tenzing Norgay, a climber and his Sherpa, reached the peak. At the time, Tenzing Norgay was the most experienced Everest veteran alive, having participated in six previous attempts to summit starting in 1935.

Hillary and Norgay were celebrated across the world for being the first to complete the Everest climb but there is some debate as to whether or not they were the first to reach its peak. In June of 1924, nearly 30 years earlier, George Mallory and Andrew Irvine were only 800 feet from the top when they were last seen alive by fellow climber, Noel Odell. He saw them just as they were surmounting an obstacle on the Northeast Ridge and described them as "going strong for the top." They were never seen alive again.

For years, the world wondered if they actually made it to the top but when Hillary and Norgay reached the summit in 1953 they found no signs that anyone had been there before. It wasn't until 1999 when Mallory's body was found, well-preserved from the cold, that speculation began again. Mallory had suffered a serious fall that broke his leg and caused a serious wound to his skull but additional evidence was discovered that caused many to believe that the fall occurred after they had summited Everest. The body was discovered at a lower altitude than they were last seen and was only an hour or two from the safety of their camp. In Mallory's pocket was found a pair of goggles, suggesting he was descending at night when he fell. Also, the photograph he carried of his wife and had planned to place on the summit was not found among his remaining personal possessions.

When Hillary spoke about his climb and the possibility that Mallory had beat him to the top he said, "I do not know whether Mallory and Irvine reached the summit. What I do know is that Tenzing Norgay and I were the first to get to the top and back down to the bottom again. I have always felt that you haven't completed the job on the mountain until you get safely to the bottom again." This statement has proven portentous.

A lot of people think that climbing Mount Everest is one of the hardest challenges in the world, but that's not quite accurate. It's the final part of the ascent and then coming back down that have proven to be the most dangerous. From 1921-2014, Everest has been scaled by more than 5,000 people and at least 260 have lost their lives, making the odds of not surviving the climb about 1 in 20. But of all the deaths, only 15% happened on the way up or before leaving the final camp. Nearly 85% of the deaths on Everest have happened near the top or on the way back down to base camp. It's called the "death zone" for a reason.

Near the peak of Everest, the altitude starts to take a terrible toll and combined with the cold and the physical strain the combination is brutal. Those who have made the climb talk about the incredible effort required during the final ascent and descent, noting the hypothermia, fatigue, cerebral edema, and frostbite, all the while stumbling through the dark on the way back down. After spending all your energy and strength and oxygen reserves getting to the top, you must then navigate and negotiate your way carefully back to base camp. On the way back down the peak is just as steep, the rocks just as treacherous, the ground just as slippery, the crevasses just as deep, but now you have been climbing for over 20 hours and you are weak and tired and cold.

Making it to the top of Everest is a great achievement but it's only celebrated if you get back down. The same goes for retirement. Getting *to* retirement is only half the job. All the effort to save and build your nest egg only gets you to the starting line. A one-way trip doesn't count. No matter how well you have done preparing and ascending your retirement mountain, you still have to navigate your way through the years of retirement, carefully executing a well-planned descent. As Hillary succinctly said, "You know what, I think the coming-down part is also rather important."

Reasons for success

In Edmund Hillary's autobiography, he writes about the reasons the expedition was ultimately successful. He notes four things that made the difference: the work of previous expeditions, detailed planning, excellent tools and equipment, and experienced Sherpas. These same keys will allow you to successfully navigate your own retirement journey.

"Previous expeditions"

Hillary noted that "other expeditions did not fail; they made progress." Luckily, you are not the first person who has ever had to navigate retirement. You can learn a lot from the mistakes of others and adjust your plan accordingly. A good example of this is the 4% rule which used to be the gold standard for withdrawal rates from retirement accounts. Over time we have learned that in many cases this withdrawal was too high and people still following it are running dangerously low on funds. As a result, you can make sure to avoid this mistake during your descent.

Another example is the false sense of security average rates of returns give in estimating the longevity and potential growth of your money. Previous "expeditions" have shown the consequences of not accounting for sequence of returns risk and the difference that actual vs. average returns can make on your account balances. Understanding the mistakes of those that have gone before you will allow you to steer clear of the same pitfalls during your retirement.

"Solid, thorough, meticulously detailed planning"

Hillary used three adjectives—solid, thorough, meticulously detailed—to describe the intense planning that went into the

1953 expedition. He and the other climbers on his team spent over a year planning their climb. They left nothing to chance. They planned their route, they planned for contingencies, they planned where they would camp, how they would traverse the ice falls, and where and when they would use their oxygen reserves. In fact, in the original plans it was not Hillary that was designated to summit the mountain but other climbers on the expedition. But because they had made contingency plans for illness, fatigue, and setbacks, they were still able to have someone on the expedition summit the mountain on that day in May.

A similarly detailed and comprehensive plan is needed to safely navigate your retirement. Remember, you really only get one shot at this so you want to be prepared. A comprehensive retirement plan will include a detailed income plan, strategies for when and how you will access your tax-deferred and non-qualified accounts, how to maximize your Social Security benefit, and what to do in the face of market downturns.

There is power in having a plan. Leave nothing to chance. Plan for the "what ifs." Develop a properly allocated investment strategy that will give you loss diversification strategies so you are prepared for negative changes in the market and ensure insulation against unnecessary risk. Each retirement dollar should have a purpose and be invested accordingly. Then when the time comes to use it, it's ready to be put to work.

"Excellence of equipment and tools"

A key advantage Hillary's 1953 expedition had over previous expeditions was the superior equipment and tools they had access to. Hillary's expedition was equipped with what was, at that time, state-of-the-art equipment and Hillary attributed part of their success to this improved technology. Today, the technology and equipment mountaineers have access to makes the equipment used by Hillary's expedition look like relics resulting in more and more climbers reaching the summit and returning successfully.

By comparison, there have never been more options to properly design a financial plan than we have today. Access to information is at our fingertips and investment vehicles have evolved and improved dramatically. Never have individual investors had more access to different types of investments and never have the fees and costs of investing been lower. But for all of the improvements that have been made, it is still up to you to take the steps to build a comprehensive financial plan that takes advantage of these options.

The key is to pick the right tool or investment to solve the problems you foresee. There is a time to use an ice pick and there is a time to use a rope or a ladder. You could have the very best equipment but if you use it for something it wasn't designed for the results are likely to be less than stellar. For example, if you need income in retirement, use the strategies that are designed to produce income efficiently. If volatility and risk are making it hard to sleep at night, reallocate your funds into investments with guaranteed growth options. If fees are eating away at your returns, work at reducing their footprint. Every piece of equipment on Hillary's expedition had a purpose. The same goes for the investment options inside your retirement plan.

"The work of the sherpas"

Hillary was adamant that he would never have reached the peak of Everest without the help of Tenzing Norgay, his Sherpa guide. In fact, for years neither climber would say who reached the peak first because they both acknowledged that they couldn't have done it alone. Hillary was quick to recognize that "in the work of our Sherpas, lies the immediate secret of our success."

Tenzing Norgay had been part of six previous expeditions and had worked on the mountain for over twenty years. Norgay knew the mountain. He knew the terrain. And he knew how to get back down. At one point, as they were descending the ice fall, Hillary misjudged the width of a crevasse and fell. The two men were roped together and Hillary was saved by Norgay's quick thinking. The Sherpa quickly dug his ice ax into the snow and whipped the rope around it, stopping Hillary's fall and leaving him swinging against the crevasse wall.

Today, all expeditions to climb Everest include Sherpa guides. Even the most experienced climbers in the world recognize their importance. British mountaineer Kenton Cool, who has successfully climbed Everest eleven times, stated: "The Sherpas are so important...They really are the backbone of any expedition." The reason for this is the special set of skills and characteristics that make them invaluable on Everest.

The greatest danger climbers face when climbing Everest has nothing to do with the terrain or the cold but instead the low oxygen levels at high altitude. Near the summit, oxygen levels drop to dangerous levels that can lead to very serious lung and brain complications that can threaten and even kill mountaineers. Sherpas, on the other hand, have lived in the high altitudes of the Himalayas for generations which has resulted in genetic adaptation that allows them to thrive at these altitudes. Researchers have found that Tibetan highlanders do not overproduce red blood cells in response to oxygen deprivation which prevents the development of high altitude illnesses such as swelling of the lungs and brain. Their physical advantages, coupled with their extensive experience on the mountain itself, make them an invaluable asset for a successful ascent.

Just as on Everest, as you navigate the new retirement it is essential that you have an experienced guide with the skills and abilities to lead you successfully along the path and ensure the "round trip." The do-it-yourself approach to retirement is full of numerous pitfalls and mistakes and can often result in devastating conclusions. You need someone who knows the landscape, who can see the big picture, who knows where the crevasses are and can help you avoid the treacherous precipices and manage the unexpected hazards of the journey. Finding a skilled advisor, one that is held to a fiduciary standard—which means that they must put your needs ahead of their own—can be the most important decision you make as you begin retirement.

Steady now

My daughters are serious about gymnastics and I love to go watch them compete; except for one event: the balance beam. I hate watching the beam routines. I've lost years off my life watching beam routines. Of all the surfaces in sport—from the fields to the diamonds to the rinks—none is more unforgiving than the balance beam. Just ten little centimeters stand between my girls and wide open space, less than four inches separating success and failure.

On the balance beam, there is no room for error. There is beam and air and nothing else—nothing to hide behind. Small mistakes quickly become obvious and there is no way to hide the flaws of your routine on the balance beam.

Those of you nearing retirement know exactly what I'm talking about. When your income stops, the truth of your situation becomes very clear. In many ways, whether you're descending Everest, dismounting the balance beam, or navigating your retirement, it might feel like there is not that much separating you from the wide chasm of disaster. But with a plan in place, a team to help you, employing the right tools at the right time, and a knowledgeable guide leading the way and watching for hazards, you can not only navigate the new retirement, you can do it successfully and confidently.

Steady now. Take a deep breath. Take in the view and all the possibilities that lie ahead. Now, go to work!

ENDNOTES

1. Boyd, Donald J., and Yimeng Yin. *Public Pension Funding Practices*. The Rockefeller Institute of Government, State University of New York, June 2016.
2. Matthews, Chris. "California's Pension Funding Crisis Just Got Worse." *Fortune.com*, Time, Inc., 19 July 2016, fortune.com/2016/07/19/pension-underfunded/. Accessed 27 Oct. 2016.
3. Social Security Administration, Office of the Chief Actuary. *Life Tables for the United States Social Security Area 1900-2100*. By Felicitie C. Bell and Michael L. Miller, Actuarial Study no. 120, Aug. 2005. SSA Pub. No. 11-11536.
4. Kisser, Michael, et al. *Longevity assumptions and defined benefit pension plans*. 31 Dec. 2013.
5. Lynch, David J. "Bad News: People Are Living Longer; Just Ask AT&T, IBM, GM." *Bloomberg.com*, Bloomberg L.P., 9 Feb. 2015, www.bloomberg.com/

news/articles/2015-02-09/bad-news-people-are-living-longer-just-ask-at-t-ibm-and-gm. Accessed 27 Oct. 2016.

6. "General FAQs about PBGC." *pbcg.gov*, USA.gov, www.pbgc.gov/about/faq/pg/general-faqs-about-pbgc.html. Accessed 27 Oct. 2016.

7. *HIGH-RISK SERIES: An Update.* Report to Congressional Committees no. GAO 15-290, Government Accounting Office, Feb. 2015, pg 342.

8. Edelen, Roger, et al. "Shedding Light on "Invisible" Costs: Trading Costs and Mutual Fund Performance." *Financial Analysts Journal*, vol. 69, no. 1, Jan.-Feb. 2013.

9. Kalish, Jerry. "What's 1% worth?" The Retirement Plan Blog, edited by Jerry Kalish, National Benefit Services, Inc., 21 Dec. 2007, www.retirementplanblog.com/401k-plans/whats-1-worth/. Accessed 19 May 2017.

10. Finke, Michael S. and Pfau, Wade D. and Blanchett, David, The 4 Percent Rule is Not Safe in a Low-Yield World (January 15, 2013). Available at SSRN: https://ssrn.com/abstract=2201323 or http://dx.doi.org/10.2139/ssrn.2201323

ABOUT THE AUTHOR

Matt Deaton graduated summa cum laude from Arizona State University with a Bachelor of Science degree in Finance. He later returned to Arizona State and earned a Master of Business Administration degree. Matt has acquired extensive financial knowledge and has educated thousands of individuals on personal finance and  retirement strategies. He has helped hundreds of individuals and families create comprehensive retirement plans utilizing personalized strategies and tactics to enable them to retire successfully. His greatest satisfaction comes from helping his clients find solutions to their personal financial challenges and reduce their retirement anxieties.

Matt and his business partner host a weekly radio show, *Winning with Money*, and appear regularly on a morning money segment on ABC15 in Phoenix. Matt has also been featured on FOX News Live and has had several articles published on FOXBusiness.com, Fortune.com, and CNNMoney.com.

Matt lives in the Phoenix metro area with his wife and three children.

Made in the USA
San Bernardino, CA
28 June 2017